The Ladies and the Mammies

The Ladies and the Mammies
Jane Austen & Jean Rhys
by Selma James

FALLING WALL PRESS

The Ladies and the Mammies published by Falling Wall Press
First published October 1983

Printed in Great Britain by SRP Ltd., Exeter
Cover printed by Potten, Baber & Murray Ltd., Bristol
Cover design by Mark Ranshaw

ISBN 0 905046 24 2 (cased)
ISBN 0 905046 25 0 (paper)

Falling Wall Press Ltd.
75 West Street, Old Market, Bristol BS2 0BX, England

Contents

About This Book

This book grew out of a speech with the title 'Ms. Jane Austen', given at the Cheltenham Literary Festival on 4 November, 1979. My theme was the women of the Great House, first in Ms. Austen's novels and then in *Wide Sargasso Sea*, a novel written almost 150 years later by Jean Rhys, a West Indian who lived most of her life in Europe, mainly in England, and who died in 1979.

Ms. Austen's heroines are not always literally in the Great House, but they are within its ambit, as close and often poor relations, or as they eventually marry its master.

Wide Sargasso Sea takes place on both sides of the Atlantic, but the Great House remains its focus. Within and around it, Ms. Rhys's white West Indian heroine confronts the historic antagonism between herself and Black women, between 'the ladies and the mammies', an antagonism which English literature has never tackled.

I spoke at Cheltenham at noon on Sunday, when most women are at home preparing dinner. But Ms. Austen is so attractive to women that about 200 roasts were not cooked that day, probably surprising the families as much as the Festival organisers. Her readers are amazingly faithful. I've tried to find out why, and who they are. The oldest I've interviewed, Mrs. Winifred Anne Anstie, is in her nineties and still re-reading her friend. The youngest is a student in her twenties. I have learnt a great deal from these readers; they helped to shape Part I, the section on Jane Austen. Part II is on Jean Rhys.*

My major concern has been to demonstrate that Jane Austen and Jean Rhys are two of the greatest protagonists through fiction women have ever had.

Virginia Woolf compared Jane Austen to Shakespeare. After years of reading and re-reading Austen novels late at night to replenish my fighting spirit, I agree that it is a fair comparison. Virginia Woolf claims that Ms. Austen's sentence is female. There I am on shakier ground because I am not a creator of fiction and cannot hear a literary cadence as she did. But I do know that Jane Austen speaks for me, not only because she says things I want said, or because she says things I need to hear, but also because she is always saying so many things at once, much as we women perceive a thousand truths even in chance conversation — so many we don't know how many. Who else has done that for us? Very few. And Ms. Austen did it first. She broke the ground and, though she is loved, her work is often trivialised for doing it.

* I hope to make Ms. Austen and Ms. Rhys accessible to those who haven't enjoyed them yet and/or to those who know them but aren't used to reading books about books. For this reason, I tried to keep the kind of references academia demands to a minimum. All references in Part I are to the five Oxford University Press volumes of the Austen novels. For Part II, I used the André Deutsch (London 1966) edition of *Wide Sargasso Sea*, and the Popular Library (New York undated) edition of *Voyage in the Dark*, another beautiful Rhys book. The page numbers follow the quotations so there is no need to refer to the Notes for this.

Jean Rhys has a different significance. She has pushed her way into English fiction and demanded her right not only to be heard as a woman but as a Third World woman – even in the great halls, even on the battlements. Feminism and fiction will never be the same.

It was only recently that I understood that Jane Austen is not considered a 'feminist' writer, a judgement which I challenge. But I felt that to incorporate polemic might throw the script off course, would take the focus off the writers and what they say. I have therefore responded in the Notes rather than in the text. The same is true of my contribution to an ongoing debate on the conclusion of *Wide Sargasso Sea*.

I also found myself wanting to convey to readers some of the wider implications of what I was claiming for Ms. Austen and Ms. Rhys, and some connections which were for me unavoidable. They went beyond the scope of Parts I and II, so this also is now in the Notes – which I hope the reader will not treat as mere references. They contain some of my basic assumptions about writers and writing.

The word "mammy" in the title of this book may present a problem. While everyone knows – or thinks they know – what a "lady" is, "mammy" is not so familiar outside of the English-speaking New World. As with "lady", there is no one view of the meaning, but since "mammy" refers to Black women, it is here defined by a Black woman. The definition is in the Appendix, and is from *Sharpening the Mother Tongue: The New Women's Dictionary*, which is soon to be published.

The definition appears here for the first time. Even one example shows that this new way of defining words has come not a moment too soon. It is not a different process from that of relating to these great women writers. We have needed to define ourselves by reclaiming the words that define us. They have used language as weapons. When we open ourselves to what they say and how they say it, our narrow prejudices evaporate and we are nourished and armed.

I am grateful for the help of a number of people.

Wilmette Brown read and edited the manuscript which was prepared in four intensive weeks. Part of this was during her once-a-year holiday and she gave her time cheerfully. It was decisive to have her experience as a Black woman and as a poet scanning and commenting on everything as it was written. She is also a good editor. Thank you, Wilmette.

Sara Callaway and Suzie Fleming also read the manuscript. Sara's advice, given at short notice, was crucial to Part II. Suzie as usual asked embarrassing questions the answers to which made the text clearer. Thank you both.

Ruth Todasco, creator and editor of *Sharpening the Mother Tongue: The New Women's Dictionary*, gave her enthusiastic permission to publish the definition of Mammy. Thank you, Ruth.

Sam Karl Weinstein (my son), also on his annual holiday from his 80-hour week as a union president, washed quite a few dishes, prepared food, shopped, made tea, etc., to get this written. They also serve who only do the housework. His critical comments were always useful. (He's been a good literary critic since he was nine, when he taught me about *Huckleberry Finn*.) Thank you, Sam.

Jeremy Mulford always backed me, to speak on Ms. Austen and Ms. Rhys and then to write it up and publish with him. Thank you, Jeremy.

Finally, to the women of the International Wages for Housework Campaign, which teaches me so much, and which specialises in giving women the confidence to pursue the talents society denies they have, a very special thanks.

                                                        Selma James
5 September 1983   London NW2

The Ladies
and the Mammies

I

First of all, I must explain that I am not a literary critic. Yet I am presuming to speak about the work of Jane Austen, one of the most formidable and prestigious writers in English. I am encouraged in that presumption by all those who have 'democratised' literature and literary criticism. All the former British colonies – from the United States, to India, to the islands of the Caribbean – where English is the lingua franca, spoken by non-literate and literate alike, each has breathed new life into English, by stretching the language in order to express its own experience. They have created independent bodies of literature, a process that was inseparable from the birth of the national independence movements. These new literary traditions assisted in the disintegration of the ethos of an élite, sweeping away (at least in theory) the idea that there are those who are and those who are not capable of writing or criticising – or of governing.

I want to extend that 'democracy' further – against another élitism – away from professionalism, which the women's movement has done most to undermine.[1] Not only professionals have the right to be critics. Others can

profitably be heard on the subject of literature. Nor do I
believe that standards need to be lowered to 'let in' the
non-professional. A wider participation can raise standards,
can widen their scope. So that in claiming my own right to
be an occasional 'critical critic',[2] I hope to help open the
way for others to register their claims to the same right.

I have a right to speak on Jane Austen first of all
because I'm a reader, and she didn't write for literary
critics, she wrote for readers; secondly because I'm a
woman, and she was a woman writing for women. It's true
that she was writing for very few women; we have to
remember that she was writing at a time when most people
couldn't read; and also that her readers had to be from
among those few who could afford either to buy books or
to subscribe to the lending libraries she refers to in the
novels. So she was writing for a very small, very select
audience. But it was an audience largely of women. (This
seems to have been generally true of novel readers at that
time, particularly romantic novel readers. It was primarily
women's patronage — women as novel consumers — that
paid for the novel to be born and to grow.)

I have a right to speak about her in spite of the fact
that I am not of the class of her heroines: even when
they were financially dependent, they were largely in the
upper class or the middle class, the same as her readers. It
is a tribute to her genius that I have never felt this as a
barrier. Jane Austen so concentrated on what was specific
to women and therefore what all women have in common — despite the class antagonisms that divide us — that
her heroines get on extremely well with women like me.
(We are immeasurably helped, I think, by her never taking
money for granted; but more of this later.)

Now I haven't made an exhaustive study of the Austen
critics. I've concentrated on reading the novels. My ideas
are based almost exclusively on reading and re-reading the
same six books. In not having read the detailed analyses
of all the critics, I'm sure I've missed much. But my

approach also has advantages. I read the books because I loved them. And since I was excited by the view of the world that they convey, I was often overflowing about them to all my friends, quite a few of whom are not readers – they are literate, but they're more likely to read the *Mirror* than the *Guardian*, and the occasional Harold Robbins rather than Nabokov (except for *Lolita*). Luckily, they enjoyed my Austen effusions, and just loved the passages I read aloud as illustration. In this way, I was honing my perceptions by comparing them with those of people who, like me, read fiction only for pleasure and not also as a profession or even a social obligation. (Unfortunately, 'required reading' doesn't end at school.) They were delighted to know that a 'classic' need not be just another piece of hard work (being women, and not rich women, they have had enough of that!), but that it can relate to the lives they lead, corroborating their own perceptions as women, and in this way validating them. They began to urge that I do something public with what I was finding out. This, they said, is not the kind of thing we were punished with in Eng. Lit. That's when it became necessary for me to find out what some experts had to say.

On the whole, I wasn't happy with the experts I read, because they seemed to me to reduce Jane Austen to their view of what she *should* be saying, and to the support of what they think she *should* be defending. I find this unacceptable in criticism. I don't think anyone has a right to utilise the writer or for that matter any artist (or for that matter anyone) to get some point of view across that *they* have, some perception of the world that *they* have, some axe that *they* have to grind, at the artist's expense.

Now I'm a feminist and I grind the feminist axe all the time. But what I say here about Jane Austen (and later, Jean Rhys) is based as far as I can manage on what I have read in the novels. And in the course of what I will

say here, I'm going to quote from her to demonstrate what
I think she has been telling us, and what some critics have
been mishearing or trying not to hear. The reader can
judge Jane Austen for herself. Unless we concentrate on
what she is saying, detailed analysis can misinterpret, even
ignore, what is evidently there.

   Seeing Jane Austen as she is doesn't mean agreeing with
all she says. It is appropriate for me to note here that I dis-
agree with her profoundly on a fundamental matter. The
conclusion she reached in her last novel, *Persuasion*, is that
we have to make the best of the tragic circumstances of our
lives; we are not mistaken to allow ourselves to be persuaded by authority. Now I don't think we have to make
the best of it, and I don't for a second believe in giving in
to authority. I think we have to entirely transform this
society which makes our lives a tragedy. But I think she is a
great artist because she saw our lives *were* a tragedy and
that we could be much more than they allowed us to be.
May I repeat this: there is not one 'tragedy' in any of her
novels. None of the women is exploited as servant, mill-hand
or even governess, who were to become the embodiment of
exploited womanhood in 19th century literature. In addi-
tion, all the novels have happy endings. But her fury at the
polite brutality that surrounded her and her use of comic
irony to regulate her hatred[3] of much about the world she
knew, sprang from a deep and pervasive assumption that the
circumstances of the lives of her characters were tragic.

AUSTEN AND MOZART

Jane Austen is dealing first of all with the tragedy of the
division between women and men. Before I quote a passage
to that effect, I want to note that the kind of treatment
Jane Austen has received from some critics is very similar,
and for similar reasons, to the treatment that, until
relatively recently, Mozart received. They lived about the
same time (Mozart: 1756-1791; Austen: 1775-1817). And

they both – he in the operas, she in the novels – dealt with personal relations and the intrigues within the Great House. (I am using the English and West Indian term. In the southern United States it is called the Big House or just The House.)

We have to remember that the Great House, both in England and in the New World of slave times, was part of the government of the day. A lot of Western society was ruled from Great Houses. Austen in her novels, and Mozart particularly in *The Marriage of Figaro* and *Don Giovanni*, dealt with the power struggles of individuals in that institution. Mozart until the beginning of the 20th century was considered to be writing the musical equivalent of a 'comedy of manners', which is how Austen's work is characterised even now. He was considered very feminine, which – until the women's movement of today – was derogatory. Those who condemned him in this way had no idea that they were giving high (and most apt) praise. It meant he was perceiving society through the eyes of those who tend to see great social movements in terms of their own most intimate personal relationships. Not a bad thing for an artist (not really a bad thing for anybody), though this is considered naive.

It was only in the 20th century that Mozart was finally seen to be a great composer, and in my view (and I'm not unique in this) the greatest composer from the West. It is important to know this about Mozart because it shows that when Jane Austen is reduced to 'Gentle Jane',[4] she is put down not only because she is a woman – that certainly helps – but because she is concentrating almost exclusively on what happens in a household, and from the point of view of the weaker – that is to say, the less socially powerful – sex.

The question is: does what happens in households, great or small, relate to what happens in the world outside, and if so, how? When Jane Austen says to a young writer that '3 or 4 Families in a Country Village is the very thing to work on',[5] though this might encompass the crisis in the lives of the people in these families, do these people's lives tell us anything significant about the world beyond that village? Has she encompassed any of the basic facts of economic, political and/or social life generally? I believe she did and I will attempt to demonstrate it.

THE TRAGIC DIVISION OF THE SEXES

Even before we consider her biography, let's begin with what she had to say about the tragedy of the division between women and men, and what that division was like as she had lived it, observed it and artistically represented it. The book is *Persuasion*. It was her last. She was near death by the time she had finished it, in 1817, and she got herself into a terrible panic because she knew she was dying and didn't want the book to be published until she had made some changes. She replaced one chapter towards the end with two new ones which she managed to finish in time. They greatly improve the book and make her intentions clearer. I'm going to quote from one of those added chapters, and therefore from what she knew to be her last public thoughts.

The situation is that a Captain Harville had a sister who died, and that sister was engaged to marry his friend, Captain Benwick. Both men had been in the Navy and had seen action in the Napoleonic Wars. When Harville's sister died, Benwick was shattered. He grieved for some months, and then found himself in love with another woman, whom he is now going to marry. Harville is quite distraught at the idea that Benwick can so rapidly consider marrying someone else when not long before he had claimed to be so absolutely devoted to Harville's now dead sister.

Harville is talking about this with Anne Elliot, the heroine, who brings to the conversation her own experience of constancy. She had been persuaded eight years before not to marry the man she loved, and although she has not seen him or received any encouragement from him for years, she has never married and still secretly loves him. Harville is speaking about his sister:

'It was not in her nature [to have forgotten so quickly]. She doated on him.'

'It would not [Anne answers] be in the nature of any woman who truly loved.'

Captain Harville smiled, as much as to say, 'Do you claim that for your sex?' and she answered the question, smiling also, 'Yes. We certainly do not forget you, so soon as you forget us. It is, perhaps, our fate rather than our merit. We cannot help ourselves. We live at home, quiet, confined, and our feelings prey upon us. You are forced on exertion. You have always a profession, pursuits, business of some sort or other, to take you back into the world immediately, and continual occupation and change soon weaken impressions.' [Please note: 'We live at home, quiet, confined, and our feelings prey upon us.']

'Granting your assertion that the world does all this so soon for men, (which, however, I do not think I shall grant) it does not apply to Benwick. He has not been forced upon any exertion. The peace turned him on shore at the very moment, and he has been living with us, in our little family-circle, ever since.'

'True,' said Anne, 'very true; I did not recollect; but what shall we say now, Captain Harville? If the change be not from outward circumstances, it must be from within; it must be nature, man's nature, which has done the business for Captain Benwick.' [That is, if it is not the circumstances of their lives which have shaped them differently, then it must be natural for women and men to be so different from each other.]

'No, no, it is not man's nature. I will not allow it
to be more man's nature than woman's to be incon-
stant and forget those they do love, or have loved. I
believe the reverse. I believe in a true analogy between
our bodily frames and our mental; and that as our
bodies are the strongest, so are our feelings; capable
of bearing most rough usage, and riding out the
heaviest weather.'

'Your feelings may be the strongest,' replied Anne,
'but the same spirit of analogy will authorise me to
assert that ours are the most tender. Man is more
robust than woman, but he is not longer-lived; which
exactly explains my view of the nature of their
attachments. Nay, it would be too hard upon you,
if it were otherwise. You have difficulties, and priva-
tions, and dangers enough to struggle with. You are
always labouring and toiling, exposed to every risk
and hardship. Your home, country, friends, all quitted.
Neither time, nor health, nor life, to be called your
own. It would be too hard indeed' (with a faltering
voice) 'if woman's feelings were to be added to all
this.' [pp. 232-3]

In other words, it's not men's fault that they are not as
constant and as tender as women. It is in the nature of the
lives that they live. And it is not women's fault if we are
so tender. It is in the nature of the lives *we* live. And
further, it would be a terrible catastrophe if men had to
live men's lives and women's also. Which is precisely what
has happened today — to women — all of those millions of
us who go out to work every morning; who take all the
blows that men have always taken, and who then return
home in the evening to do the job that waits for us,
which requires above all our patience and our tenderness.
How can this be a solution to the tragedy of the divisions
between women and men?

Of course she is describing the life of an active

'gentleman', especially his activity in time of war; but her description goes far beyond that limited group, since even in war no 'gentleman' would have admitted to 'labouring and toiling'. We have here an example of a technique often used by Jane Austen, to slip in what she wants said — which her readers might not ordinarily accept unadorned — in a context that helps it to pass the reader's censorship because it passes the reader's notice. She broadens a statement about gentlemen to a general statement about men; as she is dying she slips in her view of the lives of men in general, most of whom are not gentlemen. So that it is not only the lives that men live but the 'labouring and toiling' — the work that they do.

She is also making a general statement about women. Certainly, to say that 'we cannot help ourselves' when we are constant, that it is 'our fate rather than our merit', describes the resignation and defeat of every woman, lady or not, who has ever been devastated in a relationship with a man and who would not or could not turn off, as men in a similar position tend to do so much more easily and quickly.

Other writers, especially if they are men, often glorify this characteristic of suffering for love and tend to put it down as natural to women.[6] In this way, women are doomed *by nature* to suffer at the hands of men, and men cannot help themselves in wronging women. Ms. Austen knows that it is a cross we would rather not bear and that it is not natural for us to respond in this way.

Now this is no comedy of manners. To ask if this profound division between the sexes is natural, is to ask if it is inevitable. She does not answer the question, but she does make clear that it arises from the sexual division of labour, which splits the society along sexual lines. To say that men and women are divided in the work that they do, in the social functions that they perform and in the places where they perform those functions, and to attribute to the divisions the differences in their responses to loving, is startling.

Ms. Austen goes further. When Captain Harville disagrees that hardship can be the cause of Benwick's inconstancy, Anne restates her point. This time she does not speak specifically about Benwick but about men in general, taking the analysis beyond reliance for proof on any particular case. This too is still ahead of much present thinking, and ultimately we will have to ask why.

A SELECTIVE BIOGRAPHY

Let us see who this remarkable woman was. She was born in 1775, one year before the American Revolution began, and she died in 1817. Thus she lived through the French and Haitian Revolutions and the Napoleonic Wars. Now she really lived through these events, though she was not a participant. Like everyone else, she would have been shaken by the upheavals in the world at that time. The slaves on both sides of the Atlantic were rebelling. But she also had a more direct connection.

The French Revolution? Her cousin by marriage was an aristocrat and had his head cut off. His widow escaped to England and came to live with her, and later married her brother. She must have heard endless stories of what it was like to be living in France at that time.

The Haitian Revolution? Her sister Cassandra, the person to whom she was always closest, was to have married a man who died on San Domingo, the island of the revolution. Napoleon's troops were there to put down the slaves and were dying like flies of fever. He died at that time; he may even have died of the same fever. He may have been involved — for or against is now irrelevant. What is more to the point is that having the future husband of her beloved sister there would have made all the Haitian happenings of intense personal concern.

Her brothers were sailors in the war against Napoleon. Her novels show she was knowledgeable about the Navy.

She would have followed the battles in the papers and her brothers' stories when they were on leave.

So she knew about these momentous events. If she did not mention most of them, and did not deal with any of them, it was because she chose not to. Why not?

First of all, as a woman it was not socially acceptable then to write about politics. She could have signed the novels with a man's name, as George Eliot later did; or with a name that was androgynous, as the Brontës did. I believe her novels were too female for that. The reader could see that she knew what only women knew, especially at that time, when men and women were so much more cordoned off from each other. So it was appropriate that she signed them 'By a lady'.

Secondly, I think the audience she aimed at selling to was similar to those who today prefer *Woman's Own* to the *Economist* — there are many more of those. She was a dependent relative and she must have wanted money of her own. She wanted to write and she also wanted to sell what she wrote. It is still no mean accomplishment to say what you want to say and yet make money. Few writers who have a radical view, as she did, succeed in combining these two, as she had begun to do by the time she died.

Further, if even she did not mention the great events, it was impossible for a woman as clever, sensitive and observant as she was to avoid being influenced by them, and it was just as unlikely for that influence to be absent from her creative work. Revolutions are notorious for allowing even non-participants — even women! — new scope for telling the truth since they are themselves such massive moments of truth, moments of such massive participation.

Jane Austen chose to write about these events in a way that was appropriate to her talent, as a woman in the middle and upper classes of English society. The French and the Haitian and the American Revolutions are certainly present in her novels. They appear as *the State under siege, the mini-State of the home*, the stately home, which houses not merely the rulers, mainly but not exclusively men, but their first subjects, their dependants, mainly but not exclusively women. Rulers and dependants are locked together there by the State's basic institution: the family. This is the most unfamiliar area in that period. Without the 'home truths' of Jane Austen's novels, we are without some crucial information about that revolutionary time and therefore some crucial information about those revolutions.

A ROOM OF ONE'S OWN

Another important biographical fact about Jane Austen is that she didn't have either of what Virginia Woolf insists are necessities for a woman to be a writer. She didn't have a room of her own.[7] She shared a bedroom with her sister Cassandra, with whom she was very intimate and whose comic talent she deeply admired, and she wrote in the common room. Very often she had to leave her writing because she was called to household duties, probably by her mother (who seems to have been amazingly self-engrossed). The story is often told in books about Ms. Austen that she would not allow a squeak in the door to the sitting-room to be oiled so that she could slip her manuscript under the blotter at the first sound of an intruder.

Virginia Woolf insists also that a woman who wants to write needs £500 a year. Ms. Austen didn't have that either, or any other steady substantial sum that was hers by right. There is evidence in her letters that once she saw the possibility of making money through her novels, she viewed their publication in a different light. She went out of her way, for example, to find out what her readers' opinions were of her novels: she did a kind of consumer research by polling family and friends and keeping a record of which plots and which heroines they liked and disliked, and why.[8]

She was not unique in wanting financial independence; we all do. But somehow when we speak of artists, dead or living, literary or otherwise, we are made to feel they were, or at least they should be, above money; money and artists' desire for it are somehow not considered an acceptable motivation for their work. It tends to be worse when the artist is a woman. Wanting money does not accord well with our image as the sex that is naturally 'the most tender'. Even if artists should be immune to the demands of filthy lucre, it does not follow that they *are*. I believe all of us should be able to be immune to it, and until all of us are, none of us – artists or philistines – will be.[9]

Time, space and money were as important to Jane Austen as to anyone else, and her lack of them I believe dictated the way she wrote, its content as well as the form of her art. I don't believe that acknowledging this belittles her. Rather, it releases her from the ivory tower where no one should be imprisoned, and makes her achievements more accessible to us in order that we may more fully appreciate them.

NECESSITY AND INVENTION

Q.D. Leavis, in a remarkable series of articles in *Scrutiny* in 1941-44,[10] has shown that in the cramped circumstances of her life, Jane Austen had to devise short cuts in the creation and development of character. She didn't have a lot of time to invent new characters, so she used the same characters over and over again. She had to be economical. Just as housewives learn to prepare minced meat in a hundred different ways (or become vegetarians) when income drops or prices rise, so she learnt to use the same material for many different effects and meanings. Ms. Leavis describes just how housewifely Jane Austen was in the use of her time and her resources. She got the most out of her leftovers (since of course a writer never uses all

she discovers in her writing at any one time, whatever her
subject). I am told that Q.D. Leavis, who herself raised
a family and ran a household, knew a great deal from
her own experience about a woman's enforced literary
economy.[11]

Jane Austen developed the skill of placing the same
type of person in different situations, perhaps in another
stratum of society, which gives an entirely new dimension
to the type, and has a kaleidoscopic effect on other types
and other situations. For example, Elizabeth Bennet of
Pride and Prejudice becomes Mary Crawford of *Mansfield
Park*. Both have independent judgement, wit, the capacity
for understanding and free spirits. But Mary Crawford is
'bad' and, unlike Elizabeth, refuses marriage without
money. To show her disapproval, Ms. Austen contrasts
Mary with Fanny, the 'good' girl, so that we may dislike
her. But we find Mary the sinner more attractive than
Fanny the saint, and we are more on her side than her
creator intended. On the other hand, Fanny, whom Ms.
Austen means us to like, is dull next to her. I think Jane
Austen learnt from this mistake. She solved the problem
with the creation of Emma, the same type as Mary and
Elizabeth, but this time a sinner capable of introspection
and of changing.

In the course of fitting her material into her time
poverty in this way, Jane Austen was probably learning
about character — the relationship between type and social
setting. While she failed with the major characters in
Mansfield Park (her only real failure), she has a great
redeeming triumph with three sisters. Two of these are
lazy, self-indulgent and lacking in will-power. They are also
beautiful to look at. One marries Sir Thomas Bertram, a
wealthy and powerful man. The other marries a ne'er-do-
well. Mrs. Price is a disaster as a wife and mother, but
Lady Bertram, her rich counterpart, fulfils her functions
very well as a decoration for the Great House and the
obedient and dependent wife of a domineering husband.

Mrs. Norris, the third sister — the 'control', so to speak, for this experiment in the relationship between individual personality and social structure — though neither well married nor beautiful, and also financially disabled by widowhood, manages admirably by focussing all her energies on organising for her needs to be met.

As in Anne Elliot's conversation with Captain Harville, Jane Austen posits the view here that human personality owes much — though by no means all — to social circumstances. It was easier to do this in the small and confined society she knew than for us in the big city with its shifting population. If we know '3 or 4 Families', we know them over generations and can sort out the relative weight of the inherited characteristics and social influences which shaped each individual. In a city the isolated individual is not so easily traceable to her/his social and biological roots. In these circumstances it is easier for individual personality to appear as 'natural', as the product of purely internal forces, even of 'will' and 'consciousness' — self-made men.

Whatever the roots of our character, Jane Austen does not for a moment relieve us of the consequences of our weaknesses and of our responsibility for confronting them. *Emma* is about that responsibility. It is also about the charity we owe to other people who show weakness, especially if we have more social power than they do. The qualities needed to live up to this code of responsibility are will-power combined with self-consciousness, self-criticism, self-knowledge, honesty. One of the main objectives of women's consciousness-raising groups of the late 1960s and early 1970s was to achieve these qualities, to understand our own motivations and those of others, and to act consciously; so as to be better able to take responsibility for our own lives, and to wrest control over them from others. Ms. Austen's concern was our responsibility to others, as part of our responsibility to ourselves. We had our own standards, and they were not to sink to the level of the standards of those who oppressed us. The concern of the groups was our responsibility to ourselves, at the expense, we hoped, of those who were oppressing us. The two are connected: both presuppose a concentration on women and that women can change themselves by their own efforts.[12] Unlike the groups, however, Ms. Austen did not have as her starting-point the view that we could change the world. But then she didn't have a movement.

THE VICTORY OF MARRIAGE

Now, all her plots revolve around women in the period of their lives before marriage. She gets them all married because this was the best thing that could happen to a woman. A woman's only alternative was to be a 'spinster', a 'maiden aunt', an 'old maid'. Miss Bates, the 'old maid' in *Emma*, spends her life divided between caring for her aged mother and worrying about her poor and unmarried niece. She talks too much, says too little, and is entirely too dependent on the friendship and generosity of her wealthier neighbours (who knew her in better days). It is not by accident that it is Emma, the only heroine with money of her own, who decides she will never marry:

> 'I have none of the usual inducements of women to marry. Were I to fall in love, indeed, it would be a different thing! but I never have been in love; it is not my way, or my nature; and I do not think I ever shall. And, without love, I am sure I should be a fool to change such a situation as mine. Fortune I do want; employment I do not want; consequence I do not want: I believe few married women are half as much mistress of their husband's house, as I am of Hartfield [her home]; and never, never could I expect to be so truly beloved and important; so always first and always right in any man's eyes as I am

in my father's.'

[Emma's young friend, Harriet, challenges her.] 'But then, to be an old maid at last, like Miss Bates!'

'That is as formidable an image as you could present, Harriet; and if I thought I should ever be like Miss Bates! so silly − so satisfied − so smiling − so prosing − so undistinguishing and unfastidious − and so apt to tell every thing relative to everybody about me, I would marry to-morrow. But between *us*, I am convinced there can never be any likeness, except in being unmarried.'

'But still, you will be an old maid! and that's so dreadful!'

'Never mind, Harriet, I shall not be a poor old maid; and it is poverty only which makes celibacy contemptible to a generous public! A single woman, with a very narrow income, must be a ridiculous, disagreeable, old maid! the proper sport of boys and girls; but a single woman, of good fortune, is always respectable, and may be as sensible and pleasant as anybody else. And the distinction is not quite so much against the candour and common sense of the world as appears at first; for a very narrow income has a tendency to contract the mind, and sour the temper.' [pp.84-5]

So it is not celibacy that contracts the mind and sours the temper, but poverty; not lack of sex but lack of money. Women aimed at marriage to avoid being the stereotypic 'old maid' − the poor woman, who also (as Emma later says) lacked the affection of the children marriage would have provided. (Emma herself has nephews and nieces, and she will 'often have a niece with me' when she is an 'old maid'. [p.86])

Somebody like Harriet might also have been concerned that a woman was considered a failure if she didn't succeed in capturing the protection of a man's income on the one hand, and in attaining the power of being mistress of her own home on the other. It was well into the nineteenth century before 'spinsters' began to find acceptable ways of refusing poverty along with marriage. The foremost figure in transforming the meaning of 'spinsterhood' (and, by the way, of widowhood: Mrs. Norris, Lady Bertram's sister, plays exactly the same role in that household as a maiden aunt) was Florence Nightingale; and she did this by winning financial recognition for the work she and other spinsters traditionally performed without visibility, acknowledgement or payment.[13] Until that change had taken place, marriage, except for women with a great deal of money of their own, was the very best thing — was the only real choice outside of the Church — for a woman of the upper class.[14]

Emma eventually discovers (among much else about herself) that she is in love with Mr. Knightley (whose sterling character is presumably in lieu of shining armour), on whom she can depend to help pursue her determination to improve her character — another (though much rarer) function of marriage. But she gets such a good man because she is so unwilling to settle for less, and *need not* settle for less.

LOVE AND MONEY

While Emma alone among Jane Austen's heroines rejects marriage (temporarily), all of them reject marrying for money. This question of whether to marry for love or money was a critical one for women and, to a lesser degree, for men. Here is the most eloquent passage on the subject in Jane Austen's work: it explores the question in depth and takes the side of love. It is from *Pride and Prejudice*, generally recognised as one of her masterpieces.

Elizabeth Bennet is a delightful, witty, independent-minded young woman, honest both with herself and with others. She is not preoccupied by men and marriage. Nor is she a prisoner of polite society. Jane Austen has her run through a wet field and appear unashamed with a muddied petticoat in a neighbour's drawing-room — a considerable break with convention for a young lady. It represents a new and important expression of the revolutionary age. Even women were beginning to consider our individuality and our spontaneous impulses, insisting that others accept us on our terms.

Elizabeth Bennet's problem is first of all financial. Her father's estate is 'entailed': it must be passed on to a male heir, and since he has no sons (Elizabeth is one of five daughters), this would make his wife and children destitute at his death. In this passage, marriage is being proposed to Elizabeth by the clergyman cousin who will inherit the property. The benefit of such a match is clear. She, her sisters and her mother would be assured a home on her father's death. One outstanding critic, D.W. Harding, described Mr. Collins as a 'comic monster'. He's certainly absurd and Jane Austen's description of his absurdity is certainly comic; but he is just as certainly a monster. He begins his proposal by listing his interests, his concerns and his social connections.

> 'My reasons for marrying are, first, that I think it a right thing for every clergyman in easy circumstances (like myself) [he has money, or rather he is going to have] to set the example of matrimony in his parish. Secondly, that I am convinced it will add very greatly to my happiness [whether to hers or not is irrelevant, or at least secondary]; and thirdly — which perhaps I ought to have mentioned earlier, that it is the particular advice and recommendation of the very noble lady whom I have the honour of calling patroness. Twice has she condescended to give me her opinion (unasked too!) on this subject [he refers to the woman who rules the surrounding area from the local Great House, who never waits to be asked

but gives her − usually ignorant − opinion on everything to everyone]; and it was but the very Saturday
night before I left Hunsford [his home] − between
our Pools at quadrille, while Mrs. Jenkinson was arran-
ging Miss de Bourgh's foot-stool, that she said "Mr.
Collins, you must marry. A clergyman like you
must marry. − Chuse properly, chuse a gentlewoman
for *my* sake [characteristically, she puts *her* conveni-
ence first in the matter of *his* marriage]; and for your
own, let her be an active, useful sort of person, not
brought up high, but able to make a small income go
a good way. This is my advice. Find such a woman as
soon as you can, bring her to Hunsford, and I will
visit her." Allow me, by the way, to observe, my fair
cousin, that I do not reckon the notice and kindness
of Lady Catherine de Bourgh as among the least of
the advantages in my power to offer. [He's offering
his "patroness" as the second reason why Elizabeth
should marry him.] You will find her manners
beyond anything I can describe [and as the novel
unfolds, they are beyond anything that *anybody*
could describe]; and your wit and vivacity I think
must be acceptable to her, especially when tempered
with the silence and respect which her rank will
inevitably excite. Thus much for my general intention
in favour of matrimony; it remains to be told why my
views were directed to Longbourn [Elizabeth's home]
instead of my own neighbourhood, where I assure
you there are many amiable young women [I'm
doing you a favour in even considering you for
marriage]. But the fact is, that being, as I am, to
inherit this estate after the death of your honoured
father, (who, however, may live many years longer,)
[but it will be most inconvenient if he does] I could
not satisfy myself without resolving to chuse a wife
from among his daughters, that the loss to them
might be as little as possible, when the melancholy

event takes place — which, however, as I have already said, may not be for several years. This has been my motive, my fair cousin, and I flatter myself it will not sink me in your esteem. [In other words, his self-esteem, for his own generosity, could not be higher.] And now [as an afterthought] nothing remains for me but to assure you in the most animated language of the violence of my affection. [The violence of his affection: this *is* believable.] To fortune I am perfectly indifferent [he has shown that money doesn't matter to him at all], and shall make no demand of that nature on your father [he will not ask him for a dowry of any kind — because he is generous? Not at all:], since I am well aware that it could not be complied with; and that one thousand pounds in the four per cents. which will not be yours till after your mother's decease, is all that you may ever be entitled to. On that head, therefore, I shall be uniformly silent; and you may assure yourself that no ungenerous reproach shall ever pass my lips when we are married.' [He won't remind her that she's poor. A man like him, however, can be counted on to remind her that he is not reminding her.]

It was absolutely necessary to interrupt him now.

'You are too hasty, Sir,' she cried. 'You forget that I have made no answer. Let me do it without farther loss of time. Accept my thanks for the compliment you are paying me. I am very sensible of the honour of your proposals, but it is impossible for me to do otherwise than decline them.'

'I am not now to learn,' replied Mr. Collins, with a formal wave of the hand, 'that it is usual with young ladies to reject the addresses of the man whom they secretly mean to accept, when he first applies for their favour; and that sometimes the refusal is repeated a second or even a third time. I am therefore by no means discouraged by what you have just said, and shall hope to lead you to the altar ere long.'

'Upon my word, Sir,' cried Elizabeth, 'your hope is rather an extraordinary one after my declaration. I do assure you that I am not one of those young ladies (if such young ladies there are) who are so daring as to risk their happiness on the chance of being asked a second time. I am perfectly serious in my refusal. — You could not make *me* happy, and I am convinced that I am the last woman in the world who would make *you* so. — Nay, were your friend Lady Catherine to know me, I am persuaded she would find me in every respect ill qualified for the situation.' [And when they meet, she does!]

'Were it certain that Lady Catherine would think so,' said Mr. Collins very gravely — [he almost reconsiders, but then —] 'but I cannot imagine that her ladyship would at all disapprove of you. And you may be certain that when I have the honour of seeing her again I shall speak in the highest terms of your modesty, economy, and other amiable qualifications.' [Modesty, economy — not exactly what Elizabeth considers her most important 'qualifications'. Especially as she doesn't want the job!]

'Indeed, Mr. Collins, all praise of me will be unnecessary. You must give me leave to judge for myself, and pay me the compliment of believing what I say. I wish you very happy and very rich, and by refusing your hand, do all in my power to prevent your being otherwise. In making me the offer, you must have satisfied the delicacy of your feelings with regard to my family, and may take possession of Longbourn estate whenever it falls, without any self-reproach. This matter may be considered, therefore, as finally settled.' And rising as she thus spoke, she would have quitted the room, had not Mr. Collins thus addressed her,

'When I do myself the honour of speaking to you

next on this subject I shall hope to receive a more favourable answer than you have now given me; though I am far from accusing you of cruelty at present, because I know it to be the established custom of your sex to reject a man on the first application, and perhaps you have even now said as much to encourage my suit as would be consistent with the true delicacy of the female character.'

'Really, Mr. Collins,' cried Elizabeth with some warmth, 'you puzzle me exceedingly. If what I have hitherto said can appear to you in the form of encouragement, I know not how to express my refusal in such a way as may convince you of its being one.'

'You must give me leave to flatter myself, my dear cousin, that your refusal of my addresses is merely words of course. My reasons for believing it are briefly these:— [And now the comedy ends because the power that backs the absurdity and stupidity asserts itself — the monster rears its ugly head.] It does not appear to me that my hand is unworthy your acceptance, or that the establishment I can offer would be any other than highly desirable. [I offer you status and money. You *must* want these. You *need* these to avoid misery.] My situation in life, my connections with the family of De Bourgh, and my relationship to your own, are circumstances highly in my favour; and you should take it into farther consideration that in spite of your manifold attractions, it is by no means certain that another offer of marriage may ever be made to you. Your portion is unhappily so small that it will in all likelihood undo the effects of your loveliness and amiable qualifications. [Whatever your qualifications, they mean nothing if you *don't have money*. The monster is telling the truth and trying to bring her to heel with it.] As I must therefore conclude that

you are not serious in your rejection of me, I shall
chuse to attribute it to your wish of increasing my
love by suspense, according to the usual practice of
elegant females.'

Here the reference to the 'practice of elegant females' has a
less comic meaning. He is now describing elegance as a
fashionable way of hiding the economic considerations on
which marriage is based. Elizabeth is refusing such calculations and thus has no need for such a cover. She replies:

'I do assure you, Sir, that I have no pretension
whatever to that kind of elegance which consists in
tormenting a respectable man. I would rather be paid
the compliment of being believed sincere. I thank you
again and again for the honour you have done me in
your proposals, but to accept them is absolutely impossible. My feelings in every respect forbid it. [Let's
repeat that sentence: it's extremely important because
it conveys a view still new then, and one we're
increasingly articulating today. My feelings — what I
feel, not what I own, not what rung in society I'm
born on, but my feelings — in every respect forbid
it.] Can I speak plainer? Do not consider me now as
an elegant female intending to plague you [or fool
you or manipulate you], but as a rational creature
speaking the truth from her heart.'

Here is a woman claiming to be a 'rational creature' and
demanding to be believed to be one. This must have been
quite sensational in 1813. But Mr. Collins has one more
weapon to make Elizabeth comply with his wishes:

'You are uniformly charming!' cried he, with an
air of awkward gallantry; 'and I am persuaded that
when sanctioned by the express authority of both
your excellent parents [whom, he is saying, you
will be forced to obey], my proposals will not fail
of being acceptable.' [pp. 105-9]

Whether you like it or not. What begins by being merely comic is steadily transformed without alteration of style into deadly seriousness. Mr. Collins's voice has gained an edge of confident sadism by the end. An absurd proposal of marriage by a ridiculous man to a charming and witty woman becomes a struggle of spiritual life and death between them, in which the man is backed by the power that rules society. Mr. Collins is threatening her that, irrespective of her feelings, her parents are in charge of her actions.

It was to escape that parental domination that women got married and still do, hoping for more space and more individual autonomy from their husbands than from their fathers. Even a monster like Mr. Collins had advantages, which is why the clever Charlotte Lucas marries him, to Elizabeth's astonishment. It is worth recalling, especially to feminists who may have forgotten, the traditional power of the wife. Emily Dickinson, who, like Jane Austen, never married, knew exactly what she was giving up and described the status that marriage bestowed:

> I'm 'wife' — I've finished that —
> That other state —
> I'm Czar — I'm 'Woman' now —
> It's safer so —[15]

Luckily for Elizabeth, although her mother says she will never speak to her again if she doesn't marry Mr. Collins, her father tells her 'I will never speak to you again if you *do*.' And since her father is the head of the household, 'Elizabeth could not but smile . . .' She escapes from the monster.

But Jane Austen's point remains. People, and most especially women, who want to follow their feelings are prevented from doing so, a theme which she develops through her novels. The young unmarried woman is accountable to her parents, on whom she is financially dependent, in her choice between love and money. Among other reasons for this, all her family may be deeply affected by whether she moves up or down financially through marriage. It was not a simple decision then, and even now it is less straightforward than appears. On the one hand, the society was beginning to accept, even promote, romantic love, encouraging women in the morality that ensures that our decisions are not venal: it is wrong to be materialistic; marry the man you love even if it pauperises you. On the other hand, if you don't marry for money, your family may suffer, and your first obligation is to them: there can be no morality based on the selfish consideration of your own feelings to the exclusion of their effects on others. The woman trying to live by Christian principles is confronted by two conflicting sets of principles conveyed by Christians (including clergymen like Mr. Collins). In that case, she must decide what is right for her; and Ms. Austen's novels would have been received as a contribution to that decision. In the course of deciding what is right, it was logical for a woman to develop also a sense of *her rights*, to develop her own values, and demand to live by them rather than at the mercy of the feelings and calculations of others. Elizabeth Bennet's refusal of Mr. Collins was an instance of that.

Most real life Elizabeth Bennets would have been forced to submit to the monster. Elizabeth escapes the consequences, but her action is no less brave, no less autonomous, no less bold and rebellious, for that. It was a bold thing to write and a bold thing for daughters to read. It is the comic gift which enabled Ms. Austen to pose serious problems and avoid their drastic consequences. Those who wish to turn the creator of this monster into Gentle Jane are able to hide the rebellious meaning of the action behind the lack of consequences.

Each of the women in Jane Austen's novels who wants to marry for love finds herself in some collision with her family, or, in the case of both *Sense and Sensibility* and *Northanger Abbey*, with the family of the man who is

ready to marry the poor heroine. But while all the heroines hold on to love at all costs, those who insist on
examining the finances of a match are not necessarily
stupid or malicious. There were genuinely two sides to the
question. Mrs. Jennings in *Sense and Sensibility* puts the
other, practical point of view, the one we still hear in our
own time; based not on deprivations the family will suffer
but on the fate of the lovers:

> 'Wait for his having a living! — aye, we all know how
> *that* will end; — they will wait a twelvemonth, and
> finding no good comes of it, will set down upon a
> curacy of fifty pounds a year, with the interest of his
> two thousand pounds, and what little matter Mr.
> Steele and Mr. Pratt can give her. — Then they will
> have a child every year! and Lord help 'em! how poor
> they will be! — I must see what I can give them
> towards furnishing their house . . .' [pp. 276-7]

Now that is the major theme that shapes the plot of every
one of the novels. Marriage and the dilemma of choosing
between love and money, between one or the other essen-
tial of happiness, is the perfect subject for stripping layer
after layer from the appearance of family life. Jane Austen
lays bare the heart of society: the family ruled by money.

MONEY AND THE RULING CLASSES

Jane Austen's novels centre on the conflicts over money:
the choices it opens or closes, the power it holds, and the
effects of this power on personality and relationships.
She is not coy and oblique about cash as she is about
sex. Most of her novels begin by spelling out on the first
page the financial position of families or individuals she
is introducing. The only explanation for this forthrightness
— which would usually be disapproved of as too 'materialistic' in a modern novelist — is that people around her
were open about money and its pervasive influence in a

way that we are not now. It is also possible that those with money have always been and remain that open, and that only we who lack it and are ashamed of our lack — perhaps fearing it is a mark of inferiority — only we are too reticent to be blunt about the obvious and the basic.

Ms. Austen was writing about the ruling classes. There were fundamentally two: those who ruled on the land, and those who ruled in the city. Both would have looked across the Channel and have seen that the heads of their French counterparts were being dealt with by the guillotine. The guillotine would have made people aware that something was terribly wrong with a society governed by people like Mr. Collins and Lady Catherine De Bourgh. Later in the century, Thomas Arnold, who laid new foundations for educating men of the ruling class, summed up the danger in the continuing rule of the people Ms. Austen was so accurately describing. They were a 'tribe of selfish and ignorant lords and country squires and clergymen, who would irritate the feelings of the people to madness.'[16]

But already at the beginning of the nineteenth century, Ms. Austen's readers — either those in the upper classes or those among the elevated servants (librarians, governesses, and so on) of those classes — would have felt the threat of the attack against them not only in France but on the other side of the Atlantic. They would have been trying to discover how to avoid that fate. They would have read Jane Austen's books as one reads a survival handbook.

But, for Jane Austen, the chaos was not merely external. Those who ruled society were already irritating her, and many within their own families, to madness. And although no servant has a developed personality in any of the novels, it is clear that the behaviour of the vulgar and greedy upper class towards dependent and penniless relations, from wives to cousins, was an indication of how they treated the people beyond their families, those whom they enslaved on their land and in their factories with or without wages.

I cannot, and do not, claim that she wrote her novels to educate people. But the effect of her novels must have been to educate some people. Some may have learnt from her how to handle and hold power over others. But I suspect that most of the women who have been her faithful fans from that time up to today have been reading her novels to get help in sorting out a code, a compassionate standard by which to live and to understand one's feelings in an unjust and money-dominated world. We have come to her for that because she articulates and makes novels out of the perceptions that 'we who live at home' depend on.

MARRIAGE AND THE FAMILY

Jane Austen's novels would be moralistic if they were not also examining the institutions that frame women's lives. Through the great range of women and situations she describes, it is women who are dependents who — at best — are forced to bear the brunt of the greed, vulgarity and self-indulgence that are institutionalised in marriage and the family. At worst they are entirely thwarted and their lives destroyed. In this sense she belongs in the present feminist movement, which began *not* as an attack on men but in opposition to the institution of the family. The critique of men was founded on their dominant position there. It was *institutionalised sexism* that was the enemy. It was marriage and the family that subordinated women to men and which functioned as the basis of the repression of all the individuals, including men, trapped financially and emotionally within them. Ms. Austen's novels support that view. Let us run through her heroines' families, especially the parents.

There's General Tilney of *Northanger Abbey*: he's a tyrant and we will return to him later.

The heroine's mother in *Sense and Sensibility* is widowed and poor; the heroine's brother inherits the estate. In a few unforgettable pages, this weak and greedy man is convinced by his even greedier wife not to give the widow, his step-mother, what he promised his father on his deathbed he would give her.

Mr. and Mrs. Bennet of *Pride and Prejudice* don't agree about Elizabeth marrying Mr. Collins, and they don't agree on anything else either. Mrs. Bennet is described as 'a woman of mean understanding, little information and uncertain temper'. She doesn't like her daughter Elizabeth. Mr. Bennet, who loathes his wife, seems to be in love with Elizabeth. Given the age and the audience she was trying to attract, Jane Austen was necessarily coy about sex, but she was not unsophisticated. She would have seen many disastrous marriages, though they were not called that when there was no possibility of divorce. In the same way, the sexual love of parent for child and vice versa has always been much more common than its stigma allowed, and allows, society to admit. (Mr. Bennet is not a rapist and is in no way sexually threatening to his daughter.)

Whereas Mrs. Bennet knows that her job as a mother is to work at marrying off her five daughters, so that they are set up financially, Mr. Bennet has to be nagged by his wife to do his part as a father in finding husbands for the girls. Because his wife is silly, because he hates her, and because he is lazy, he refuses to co-operate in accomplishing what is their joint responsibility. With Mr. Collins this works to Elizabeth's advantage. (Mr. Bennet backs Lizzie's refusal.) With the man she herself finds to marry, silly mother and lazy father both hinder the final matchmaking.

Mr. Bennet is incapable of governing his family. He refuses to lead. But he is in charge.

Sir Thomas Bertram, in *Mansfield Park*, is a slaveholder and Member of Parliament, probably from a rotten borough. Because there are no slaves in *Mansfield Park*, it is possible for the reader to comfort herself that this is not a political novel, that it is 'not about slavery' — unless you know that, since it is about a slaveholder, it *has* to be about slavery. Sir Thomas is an absentee owner. He owns plantations in Antigua in the West Indies. What I first understood when I read Jane Austen is that an absentee owner is absent from two places. He is absent from his plantation holdings, but is also often absent from home. Rebellion grows as soon as his back is turned: he goes to Antigua to see about all those rebellious slaves; and then he comes home and has to deal with the rebellion of those he represses and depresses in his own household, in his own family. And they do rebel. Both his daughters 'go bad'; run away to live with or marry whom they please, which was the height of immorality for that class at the time. His son, who is going to inherit the estate, almost dies from his own excesses. By the end of the novel Sir Thomas, the well-mannered tyrant, is aware that he is a failure as a father and as the ruler of his clan.

Can forced marriage and repression within the slaveholder's family be compared with chattel slavery? Is Jane Austen making such a comparison? No, not a comparison, but a connection. It would be a miracle if the slaveholder expressed his violence and cruelty in only one area. The political effect of such a narrow view is to pull slavery out of history, and to reduce it, and the racism that justified it, to a historical accident, rather than to see it for what it was, an earlier version of the society we now inhabit. The effect of dismissing as unimportant what Jane Austen says women of the slaveholding class had to bear at the hands of the master is to dismiss the attack on the slaveholder that came from within his family.[17]

Mr. Woodhouse, the father of Emma, is again ineffectual, but means no harm to anyone. A self-engrossed hypochondriac and an enormous burden of work for his daughter (he is a widower). But he is harmless. He is the titular head of the household, but it is his daughter who runs things.

Sir Walter Elliot, Anne's father in *Persuasion*, is a vain and selfish man. He spends most of his time looking in the mirror and in *Debrett's*, comparing his looks as well as his status with those of other men. Others pay for his squandering of the family fortune to feed his vanity and snobbery. He doesn't tell Anne what to do; he is not interested enough in her to tell her anything. Besides, he has nothing of value to say. Anne, like Emma, and like Mrs. Bennet, provides the leadership from behind that the family needs to survive.

FEMINISM AND MEN

Jane Austen is very clearly not saying that all men who are in charge of the households and the money are tyrants who insist on imposing their tyrannical will. But by the very fact of being heads of households, they impose their will. If they are weak, they impose their *weakness* upon you. It is not the strong and wilful men who are indicted; it is not the indecisive or lazy men who are indicted. The indictment is of men's position in the household, and of the hierarchical structure of the family. She wasn't any mean and narrow-minded ideologue, charging that all men are tyrants. What she described was how men are put in a *tyrannical position*, at least in their own homes, and sometimes over others outside. Whether they aim to tyrannise or not, even their refusal to take a dominant role is an imposition. Jane Austen's was a very big mind, a very creative mind, a truly feminist mind, it seems to me.

Hers is a most compassionate reading of human behaviour, and particularly of men's behaviour. Though it does not relieve men of responsibility — in her code we are all always responsible for all that we do or do not do — it does relieve them of blame and guilt for what is not their fault; they are not personally responsible for the power that society, through the economics of marriage and the family, has delegated to them over us; *only for what they do with it*. But if the institution is not to blame, then men are 'bad', maybe not even salvable. The latter is a view held more widely within the current women's movement than is good for us.

Jane Austen demands your sympathy even for Sir Thomas, slaveholder and defeated patriarch. I didn't expect or want to have sympathy. But she makes the case that he means well and *after getting blows* he learns to mean better. He is separated from those, even those in his own household, whom he rules — by the fact that he rules them. His character is shaped by that power, as are his relationships in the family: his daughters always contrive to have their own way behind his back. He is a pathetic figure by the end, defeated by unexpected forces, startled by something where he thought he was safest. He might be a different and better person if only he did something else, anything else but govern society.

The only head of household in all her novels whom Jane Austen entirely approves is the good-tempered clergyman, Mr. Morland, the father of young Catherine in *Northanger Abbey*. At least we think he is decent because he hasn't much money and power and he remains a subordinate character, never tested with a conflict of interests. *Northanger Abbey* is dominated by another version of Sir Thomas, General Tilney, who does not share Sir Thomas's self-discipline. No matter. The effect on the households they run, on all the people in their power, is basically the same. Something was rotten in the State of England, because something was terribly wrong with that much economic and social power being vested in the hands of any individual over any other individuals. That is certainly my view, and one I am led to by Ms. Austen's evidence. Whatever her view about power in general — whether she would have believed, for example, that it was wrong for any individual (such as the President of the United States)

to have the power over life and death for millions of
people because his finger was on the trigger — we have no
way of knowing it. But in her description of the way that,
within the household, power distorts the personality and
creates a fathomless gulf between the rulers and those
whom they rule, there is certainly ammunition for those
of us who feel that way.

THE TRAFFIC IN WOMEN

Jane Austen studiously avoided the struggle of classes
within the Great House and generally. Her focus was the
clash between those for whom love rather than cash was
supposed to be the nexus. Only once, when marriage is
unlikely, is a job discussed. At that time, the only job open
to women of the classes about whom she writes was the job
of governess. In *Emma*, Mrs. Elton (of whom more later)
urges Jane Fairfax to begin applying to be a governess, a
job she will ultimately have to do to support herself. Jane
Fairfax describes the special employment offices for that
occupation:

> 'Offices for the sale — not quite of human flesh —
> but of human intellect.' [p.300]

Mrs. Elton is shocked at the comparison and the reference
to the slave trade, and Jane replies:

> '. . . governess-trade, I assure you, was all that I had
> in view; widely different certainly as to the guilt of
> those who carry it on; but as to the greater misery of
> the victims, I do not know where it lies.' [pp.300-1]

This is the only overt condemnation of slavery in any of
Ms. Austen's novels.
    By the time this comparison between the slave-trade
and the governess-trade was written, Blake's 'dark, satanic
mills' had already established themselves. The comparison
would have had these echoes among her audience. But I

think it served another purpose.

We have already noted the way Jane Austen avoided any direct reference to sexual intimacy. Here I suggest is a case in point. Every woman would have known that slavery meant not only work on the cotton or sugar plantation from sunup to sundown, but the lack of sexual ownership of their own bodies. A governess worked and lived in a Great House virtually at the sexual disposal of the wealthy master. By evoking images of the slave-trade, which would have been current, Ms. Austen is making a bold reference to the rape that Jane Fairfax is liable to suffer as a governess — what is now called 'sexual harassment at work'.

What Jane Austen was quite straightforward about was where men's power over women — and all social power — came from. It came from money. It was money that ruled the world. Those who had money had power over those who didn't, and those who didn't were likely to be women.

Often women had to marry for money because parents forced them to. Often women chose to marry if not for money then without love because that was the only chance of gaining the *relative* financial independence that marriage alone offered women.

In fact, Ms. Austen was careful to hint only once at a tyrant husband (General Tilney in *Northanger Abbey*); so much were the structure of her novels and her happy Hollywood endings dependent on marriage holding out real possibilities for women, that she had to soft-pedal the dangers of marrying tyranny.

It is fashionable nowadays, at least in some circles, to pretend that we can rise at will above financial considerations in our personal relations. When we are stricken with such a fantasy, a dose of Austen practicality will quickly purge us back to reality. Our relations are still mediated by money; and willing this to change is not, unfortunately, enough to change it.

One of the reasons women were coerced into marrying for money at that time was that such matches were a very important part of the accumulation of capital. As long as individuals with personal fortunes, and not impersonal multi-national corporations or the State itself, were the guardians of accumulated social capital, an individual marriage could be instrumental in deciding the fate of technological development, imperial conquest, whole branches of industry. It was the impersonal arrangement of marriages that helped the progress of the Industrial Revolution that was to succeed Jane Austen, and which writers who followed her were to chronicle. She was merely dissecting the society and the classes in which big money was fought over; exploring how it felt to be a woman when not only those in the factory or in the field, but also the daughters of the Great House were the sacrificial lambs on the altar of accumulation.

MS. AUSTEN'S OWN LITERARY CRITICISM

Some of Jane Austen's audience would have been women like that, and her view of how and why they read novels was important to her theory of literature. She made this theory central to the plot of *Northanger Abbey*. It may have come quite early in her writing, though it is hard to say since she worked on her books over years, writing and re-writing. It was published after her death; but it was probably first drafted just after the first version of what was to become *Pride and Prejudice*, in about 1798. Whenever it was written, this book generally makes me feel that it was devoted to its author finding out what she should be doing by finding out what others had done, and how they had been not so much understood as emotionally received by their readers.

Northanger Abbey is usually described as a send-up of the Gothic novel — of the melodramatic novel about daughters being locked up in cellars, wives being chained, etc. − which was very popular with women readers. The heroine − an honest, good-natured but naive young woman − half-believes everything she reads in such novels. She is invited by the sister of the man she loves to be a house guest in their family home. With her head full of the fantastic plots of the Gothic novels that she regularly reads, she completely misunderstands what is happening around her. She convinces herself that the father, General Tilney, has either murdered his wife or is keeping her imprisoned somewhere in the Abbey. She is terrorised by her own fantastic enlargements of insignificant details. Catherine has been taken in by the novels at which Jane Austen leads us to believe she is poking fun.

General Tilney is behind the invitation to Catherine because he presumes that she comes from a rich family. When he discovers that she doesn't, he is so angry at his own mistake that he humiliates her by kicking her out of the house. Jane Austen now catches us entirely unawares by her very respectful description of her feelings:

> Catherine, at any rate, heard enough to feel, that in suspecting General Tilney of either murdering or shutting up his wife, she had scarcely sinned against his character, or magnified his cruelty. [p. 247]

The implication is that the emotions excited in the reader by the Gothic novel are not so very far removed from the emotions that Catherine genuinely feels during her own much less dramatic life. And she isn't wrong in her assessment of General Tilney's character; only about the nature and extent of his crime.

The plots of those novels were far removed from daily life, but the emotions they gave rise to were not. As wives and daughters, women suffered fear and terror at the hands of men like General Tilney, whether they were murderers or not. (And his son and daughter do in this novel.) We also have to bear in mind that at least some of the Gothic plots must have been based on real events. Women could not own or control their own property if they were married, which (as we shall see) opened the way for every kind of brutality. The Gothic novel may have been more of a representation of that society than at first appears.

From Catherine Morland's experience with books and life, we can gather what Ms. Austen considered was one important function of the novel; what the writer should aim at accomplishing on behalf of her readers. The writer should recreate the emotions of everyday life in the context of plot and incident that were 'safe', did not frighten the publisher or reader with a superabundance of overt subversive truth. In this way, the novel validated the emotions that it might not have been politic for women to articulate even if they had been able to find the words. The reader could then read the re-enactment of her own tragedies without being challenged to take arms against her individual sea of troubles. I am one of those women who find catharsis in such reading experience. I have always found this validation of my internal emotional life satisfying and strengthening. If no one else in the world understands how I feel, the writer does. Before the present movement, many women were dependent almost entirely on books for confirmation that their innermost thoughts and feelings were not peculiar, abnormal or absurd. Women who did not find that confirmation in books often found it in Hollywood movies, which also sought to present reality, especially to women, in a way that did not threaten – in a way that would convince us to spend our money to see them. In my experience there was more than the escapism of the happy ending to be got from many Hollywood films. Much more truth was put on the screen than intellectuals who scoffed at the popular audiences, and especially women, ever supposed.

Jane Austen makes many more currents and a much richer experience available to us than do her Gothicising colleagues. But I think she felt a deep respect for women ordinarily sneered at for reading these emotional adventure books. She showed this by affirming the right of her audience to read what they wanted to. They were, after all, in the best position to know what they needed. It was her job to find the form acceptable to them through which she could offer them her content.

At the end of her life, she gave us more of her views on writers — this time about how she took issue with them. In *Persuasion* — remember she was dying when she wrote it, and knew she was dying — the conversation quoted earlier about the differences between men and women continues. After being interrupted (for the plot to move on), Captain Harville says to Anne Elliot:

> 'Well, Miss Elliot,' (lowering his voice) 'as I was saying, we shall never agree I suppose upon this point [of the differences between men and women]. No man and woman would, probably. But let me observe that all histories are against you, all stories, prose and verse. If I had such a memory as Benwick [who is a literary man], I could bring you fifty quotations in a moment on my side the argument, and I do not think I ever opened a book in my life which had not something to say upon women's inconstancy. Songs and proverbs, all talk of woman's fickleness. But perhaps you will say, these were all written by men.' [And she says:]
>
> 'Perhaps I shall. — Yes, yes, if you please, no reference to examples in books. Men have had every advantage of us in telling their story. Education has been theirs in so much higher a degree; the pen has been in their hands. I will not allow books to prove anything.' [p. 234]

Except of course Jane Austen's. For once Ms. Austen had taken the pen into her own hands, books could begin to tell *our* story.

THE LAUNCHING OF FEMINIST FICTION

Now there seems to be a widespread opinion that feminist novelists began with the Brontës. I challenge that, not to belittle those who followed Jane Austen, but to situate her as a founder of feminist fiction. *Jane Eyre*, though tinged with racism against Mrs. Rochester and against inter-marriage,[18] certainly backs Jane's right to a life of her own. Curiously, I find *Wuthering Heights* to be strong exactly where *Jane Eyre* is weak: it is the first exploration of a relationship between a white middle class woman and a non-white (what colour is Heathcliff ?) working class man. (*Wuthering Heights* is a much finer work in other respects, too.) But in centring on women's relation to money, in making the family the focus of her attack, in defending women's right to run through fields and dirty their petticoats, to read what they please, to write books with more truth in them than men's books, to marry for love, even to refuse to marry, Jane Austen's feminism is speaking to issues which must have influenced every woman writer who followed her — *which launched feminism in fiction.*

This woman who barely mentions any big event of her time is astonishingly political. Since she is continually analysing the effects of money, she is also analysing power relations — and that by definition is politics. Furthermore, she had so worked out the dimensions of her characters' personalities that at times she indicates very clearly and devastatingly how they would react even to political issues. Mrs. Elton, a conniving, self-satisfied matron who expresses her unsavoury personality in *Emma*, responds to Jane Fairfax's remark about governessing by saying:

> 'Oh! my dear, human flesh! You quite shock me; if you mean a fling at the slave-trade, I assure you Mr. Suckling [the rich man her sister married, whose name she frequently drops] was always rather a friend to the abolition.' [p. 300]

What do Mrs. Elton's comments convey? They provide for us a picture of those who express views in favour of justice anywhere other than in the place and among the people they themselves exploit. It is Mrs. Elton who also says six pages later in the course of another conversation:

> 'I always take the part of my own sex. I do indeed. I give you notice — You will find me a formidable antagonist on that point. I always stand up for women — . . . ' [p. 306]

And since all her actions give the lie to this, we know that Jane Austen has again used Mrs. Elton to demonstrate that one should beware of hypocrites who pay lip service to fashionable causes. As the women's movement becomes more mainstream, women like Mrs. Elton find themselves attracted to its power, and use its rhetoric to gain power for themselves at other women's expense. There is already confusion about Mrs. Elton's 'feminism' among the critics.[19]

For Jane Austen, it was not enough to speak up for women, to make the right noises (though that can be extremely useful). She had to go to the source of the trouble; she had to tell the truth about the family, at least fictionally; and finally, she had to affirm and demonstrate that politics, revolution, the grasp of history, the State and its opponents, in short, the public domain and the world of men with which it had been synonymous for so long — that this world, like charity, begins at home. That is what Jane Austen attempted to do, and, considering the short time she lived and the little time she could give to writing while she lived, she did it amazingly well.

Her accomplishment in this sphere has to be measured by how difficult it is to discover and convey accurately the complicated relationship between the private and the public, between the personal and the political; and be compared with others' attempts. She chose to portray heads of households who are powerful and influential men and women in their communities. Their lives are dominated by financial considerations, by getting and spending – but mainly getting – money. Though most of her other characters accept this situation unquestioningly (and either revel in power if they have money or, if they don't, are ready to do anything to get close to those who do), others find it distasteful and are forced only by necessity to be concerned about money at all.

Jane Austen's audience would have known about the effects of these money-shaped personalities on the communities these people dominated. And she is as caustic against women like Lady Catherine De Bourgh and Lady Dashwood as she is against men like General Tilney. She was enough of a feminist to know that our case as women does not and cannot rest on the absurd view that men are bad and women are good. I would in fact go further. Our case is that we are exploited, with men the instruments and/or the beneficiaries of that exploitation.

THE PERSONAL AND THE POLITICAL

When second-rate novelists approach the exploration of the relationship between the personal and the political, either the personal swamps the political (as is the case with most biographical and political/psychological novels) or the political swamps the personal (as with socialist realism). What distinguishes a good writer from the others is the balance and integration of these two. The personal and the political, the private and the public, are and are not separate entities. We are not different people depending on whether we are in our own homes or outside; we merely display another combination of those qualities which always operate.

The novels of George Lamming of the West Indies have explored precisely the nature of the relationship between these spheres. His most concentrated and bold attempt to deal with them is *Natives of My Person*,[20] which centres on a naval Commandant, a seventeenth or eighteenth century servant of imperialism and the slave trade, who organises an expedition to break with his State and found society anew in the New World. The Commandant is able to leave the woman he loves and who loves him, in order to make repeated journeys — in order to exercise social power — even though it greatly pains her, for the same reason that he is able to consider building his utopia on captured slaves, and for the same reason that he is ultimately defeated. One does not cause the other; they are similar brutalities exercised in different spheres. His social power, over Black slaves and therefore over white wife, is the source of corruption and defeat.

If you are a woman writing at the beginning of the nineteenth century, you can make no overtly political statements, but your neighbours can work out at least some of the social and political consequences of your personal evidence. Many of Jane Austen's readers, we must remember, could see at first hand what 'great men' and 'great women' were like close up — their pettiness and vanity, their tyranny and stupidity, their lack of vision and of love — either as neighbours, employers or family. The problem is usually the accuracy of the evidence. Ms. Austen's eye and her pen are uncannily accurate and unambiguous. She gave all of her evidence under oath and never perjured herself. Social power over others stands condemned.

To label the content of this body of novels a 'comedy of manners' serves only to denigrate not merely the author but the subject of her work: women within the family.

THE HAPPY ENDING

When Jane Austen began to write, she had to learn to

temper her fury against hypocrisy and vulgarity; if the heroine is the only sensible and decent character, she will be isolated. *Sense and Sensibility* reorganises its point of view somewhere in the middle in order to create the resources for happiness for the heroine and her sister. Decent and sensible impulses are found for silly Mrs. Jennings in the second half of the book, and she is on the side of the sisters out of loyalty to other women in trouble.

But when Ms. Austen had mastered her craft, she began to knit the happy endings into the fabric of the novel from the first page. The problems she poses are not resolved in these conclusions. (In this respect again she resembles Mozart; the last movements of his piano concertos are happy and almost unrelated to the problems posed in the first and second movements.[21]) The endings are wonderful fantasies: the real-life counterparts of women like her heroines would have had far more trouble finding men to marry than they do in the novels. Each of these wonderful men is the superior of all others around him – by the end, if not at the beginning. This is in part due to Ms. Austen's preoccupation with the capacity of people – heroines or their heroes – to change themselves by working at it. It is also because she needed happy endings for her heroines and created the men who could provide them.

Yet it is almost awkward to conclude so much truth, told so caustically, with such fantasy. It may be that such conclusions mislead some critics into overlooking the crises that led to them; it is possible that the myth of Gentle Jane was born in the Cinderella conclusions without reference to anything that has gone before! But despite what they sidestep, the conclusions do bear an important relation to the rest of the books.

Jane Austen's fantasy endings were her passport to truth, her leave to enter the Great House and play her searchlight into the nasty corners. They served other purposes too. If she thought the family was a disaster, there was no alternative to the social and physical intimacy that it provided. The high level of wit and discussion within her own family helped her to develop her literary skills. Even if her mother was a self-centred hypochondriac who took the couch while her dying daughter was stretched on three chairs together, Ms. Austen was deeply dependent on the remarkably intimate relationship with her sister. She wrote more of her mind to Cassandra than to any other human being (except as this mind alchemised her feelings and impressions into the novels), and she obviously had plenty to say that was not for the eyes of anyone else. Only this can explain why Cassandra burnt most of her sister's letters after she died. She must have been dependent on Cassandra as a sounding board for ideas and impressions, and as a confidante to whom to express fears, doubts, hatreds, loves. She knew how much we needed other people. Her comic talent allowed her to pose problems and then let her heroines skip happily ever after away from them. Thus she avoided being an outcast writing about outcasts. It allowed her to write books that would sell.

While the spirit of her heroines which causes them to demonstrate some act of courage in challenging their society is never broken, the endings happily relieve them of the consequences of that rebellious spirit. I have heard the view expressed among writers that unless heroine or hero is pushed to the limit, no important truths emerge, or at least the truths that do emerge are limited; that only when characters are in the most extreme circumstances — risking their lives, for example — does fiction transcend everydayness and confront the world stripped of its mystifications. While this has its uses in fiction, and even an application in life,[22] it is a partial view which men more than women are likely to take as the whole.

Jane Austen is a brilliant novelist, which not many people are. But her raw material is very commonplace. The stuff of her novels is the perceptions and gossip of women.

You will remember Anne Elliot's words, 'We live at home, confined'; we read about the world outside on the faces of those re-entering that home. We learn to be good at reading those faces because what we read there tells us what we who have served others so long must do, and what our fate is likely to be.

Raw material is not the finished product, and Ms. Austen laboured to refine and then shape these perceptions into art. It is hard for men who are not trained to serve to appreciate how much truth is in fact available to women in our everydayness which is not available to them. They know little or nothing about how the private, the personal, the apparently undramatic, can place us in extremities at home. In that space, priorities and meanings have their own unique perspective, and it is from this perspective that Jane Austen's novels are written. It is from this perspective that all her achievements derive.

Finally, not unimportantly, last but by no means least, she wanted women to win, and her endings allow us to win. She wanted her heroines to get something for the fight they make. I am profoundly satisfied that they do: what they get is a man, in some cases a rich man, but always a good man, and always with sufficient financial prospects. Anything less would have been defeat. She wanted to say, even though you don't walk outside of society and fight from there, you have a right to victory for having fought at all. She wanted as a woman to win herself, and she won through her heroines' victories. She found a man that they could love for each of the six. Unfortunately she never found one for herself. But then we would probably have had a genius who was a wife rather than a writer.

II

Now I move from Jane Austen's English countryside in 1817 to Paris in the 1920s. During that time, many things happened to the Great House, in literature and in life.

A woman began to write in Europe, a white woman from the West Indian island of Dominica. She was discovered by Ford Madox Ford, an American novelist also living in Europe. We have to remember that until recently New World writers and artists came to Europe, especially to Paris, to be part of the artists' community there. A white West Indian would be just one more 'foreigner' who had come to the artistic mecca.

Ford was enthusiastic about Jean Rhys's 'singular instinct for form' which was 'possessed by singularly few writers of English and by almost no English women writers'. By that he meant that she could write as few men could. In fact she wrote as no men could. He was also excited that 'coming from the Antilles [she had] a terrifying insight and a terrific — an almost lurid! — passion for stating the case of the underdog . . .'[23] More than he knew, she was herself an underdog, which might explain her passion.

In the dozen or so years from the late twenties to the second world war, Jean Rhys published a book of short stories and four novels. While some of these stories are set in the West Indies, all four novels take place in Europe. With the exception of *Voyage in the Dark* (1934), the women are European and there is no hint that the writer is not European too.

But there is one thing foreign about all four of the novels. Jean Rhys's central character — whether English or Continental, and in the case of *Voyage in the Dark*, West Indian — is not a native of the country she is living in. The crisis of being an alien, an immigrant, is not the major theme, however.

These novels are about how women are aliens; how we don't stand a chance because the cards are stacked against us. The novels have in common the hopelessness and defeat and isolation of the heroine. Each personifies the female condition; each is the perfect victim, unable or unwilling to defend herself. Unable because, being a foreigner, she does not know how, since she is outside the terms of reference of the surrounding culture; unwilling because she will not fight for *things* that are withheld; or tailor her case according to what her opponent will understand and respect, but which is not the truth; or be brutally honest for the sole purpose of self-defence. Her sense of proportion is also out of kilter; she operates under a completely impractical set of priorities. These — alien set of standards, terms of reference, sense of proportion — leave the heroine vulnerable to and defence-less against domination by men and exploitation by everyone.

Her problem is most certainly not her consciousness. Nothing — neither nuance nor substantive act of social domination by men — escapes her notice. But she does not fight back. Knowing deeply what is happening and having no defence and no allies is a formula for suicide. Jean Rhys's heroines are not physically protective of themselves either.

Voyage in the Dark, the third novel, tells us that its heroine, though taken for European because she is white, is in fact a young West Indian in England. Ms. Rhys opens the book with a description of how it feels to this young chorus girl (a job Jean Rhys did too) to be in Europe, which reads like a preview of all the interviews with West Indians who came later to Britain in the forties and fifties. Anna Morgan, the heroine, is speaking in the first person. These are her first lines, and the book's:

> It was as if a curtain had fallen, hiding everything I had ever known. It was almost like being born again. The colours were different, the smells different, the feeling things gave you right down inside yourself was different. Not just the difference between heat, cold; light, darkness; purple, grey. But a difference in the way I was frightened and the way I was happy. [p.7]

Anna's age makes her more defenceless than the others, but she has always been vulnerable, since she was a child, a white child in a Black country, torn between identifying with the Black people, especially the Black women who cared for her and who sustained her, and with the white society that she inherits through her family and her race. Once she is in Europe she is cut off from Francine, the servant at home, the woman who tells her what she needs to know when her menstrual cycle begins, who nurses her when she has a fever, whom she loves more than anyone; who served and mothered her, but as a job. Thus her great love for Francine can only be expressed obliquely:

> The thing about Francine was that when I was with her I was happy. [p.57]

Anna is torn between defending her Creole mother from the charge that she was 'coloured' and desperately wishing to end her own ambiguity: she has 'always wanted to be black'.

> Being black is warm and gay, being white is cold and
> sad. [p.26]

But no one knows these things about Anna, and the
people around her wouldn't understand if she told them.
They are English, they have many crises — mainly about
money — but they seem to know who they are and who
they are not. One character tells her regularly how much
she hates 'dirty foreigners'.

Anna is kept by a wealthy man with whom she falls in
love — despite warnings from other women who also live
by being kept by men; and when he tires of her, she is
devastated. Her first response is not to leave her room or
eat or even change her clothes. ('We cannot help ourselves.
We live at home, quiet, confined, and our feelings prey
upon us.') Unable/unwilling to apply to the man for the
money he has offered, she drifts into more overt forms of
prostitution. This way of supporting herself is neither
more brutal nor more venal than the other relationships
she witnesses or herself experiences.

Anna's father is dead and Hester, her English step-
mother, makes clear that Anna's association with men
excludes her from Hester's acceptance and from the
acceptance of English Society. She traces this immorality
to Anna's affinity to Black people.

> 'I always did my best for you and I never got any
> thanks for it. I tried to teach you to talk like a lady
> and behave like a lady and not like a nigger and of
> course I couldn't do it.' [p.55]

*   *   *

Jean Rhys disappeared from view for some years. Francis
Wyndham tells us: 'The few people who remembered their
admiration for these books, and those even fewer who (like

myself) were introduced to them later and with great diffi-
culty managed to obtain second-hand copies, for a while
formed a small but passionate band. But nobody could find
her; and nobody would reprint the novels.'[24] As a result of
a radio dramatisation of one of them in the late fifties, she
was traced to Devon in the West of England. She was at
work on a new novel. It seems that 'For many years [she
was] haunted by the figure of the first Mrs. Rochester —
the mad wife in Jane Eyre',[25] the character whom we
know only from Mr. Rochester's biassed and racist
descriptions.[26]

The first Mrs. Rochester had many attractions for Ms.
Rhys from Roseau, Dominica. She too is a white West
Indian who has ended up in Europe. She is not only a
'foreigner', but the victim, the underdog personified;
entirely defined by and in the power of another, a man,
her white English husband Rochester. Charlotte Brontë's
Mrs. Rochester is the epitome of all Jean Rhys's heroines,
seen from the point of view of their tormentors. But in
her West Indian novel, Ms. Rhys sets out to tell the other
side of the story, to make Mrs. Rochester's case, to refute
the distorted account given of her by English literature.
In the process, Rochester himself gains a new dimension
and evokes in us a deeper compassion.

To accomplish this, Jean Rhys left the Europe of
Parisian cafes and London bedsits. The West Indies is no
longer a flashback or an idealisation, the internal point
of reference in her private voyage in the dark. In *Wide
Sargasso Sea*, Jean Rhys went home.

Whereas Jane Austen's heroines chose not to be outcasts, Antoinette Rochester had no choice; she was born
one. A white girl born in a Great House in a predomi-
nantly Black society, and thus cut off from the great
majority of the population except through the mistress-
servant relationship; a West Indian woman in Europe.
But to describe her as a white West Indian is also to
say that the framework of her personality, her thinking,

her attitudes, are shaped by Black people, especially by those Black girls she played with as a child, and by those Black women who raised her and nursed her in sickness and in health. In the United States this Black woman, from the time of slavery, has traditionally been called 'mammy'. Audiences internationally will know that historical figure from the absurd but celebrated movie, *Gone with the Wind*. One of the reasons that film had picket lines in front of movie theatres when it was first shown in 1939 in the United States was precisely because of its racist glorification of the mammy figure.

The title of the novel, *Wide Sargasso Sea*, is appropriate. The Sargasso Sea is in the North Atlantic and, according to the *Encyclopaedia Britannica* (1960), 'was first reported by Columbus, who crossed it on his initial "West Indies" voyage'. They also tell us that 'the widely credited story of ships becoming helplessly embedded in the floating seaweed which fill it are disproved'; but it remains a perfect image for the impenetrable and murky problems of the dark voyage between the West Indies and Europe.

So the Sargasso Sea was launched on its modern history with the first thrust of imperial conquest and the Middle Passage, the traffic in slaves. But it was party to a whole new history with what George Lamming has called 'Columbus in reverse',[27] the migration of thousands of West Indians to England, in a voyage of another kind of discovery. Mrs. Rochester had come much earlier.

Her name is Antoinette Bertha Cosway and she is born a daughter of the slave-owning class. She grows up just after the abolition of slavery, her home a white island in a hostile and rebellious Black sea. She witnesses the burning down of Coulibri, her home, by liberated Black people who are no longer disciplined by the lash.

> The house was burning, the yellow-red sky was like sunset and I knew that I would never see Coulibri again. Nothing would be left, the golden ferns and

> the silver ferns, the orchids, the ginger lilies and the roses, the rocking-chairs and the blue sofa, the jasmine and honeysuckle, and the picture of the Miller's Daughter. When they had finished, there would be nothing left but blackened walls and the mounting stone. That was always left. That could not be stolen or burned. [pp.44-5]

In every way the fire marks the end of an era.

> Nothing would be left . . . there would be nothing left . . .

Antoinette's mentally handicapped baby brother, to whom her white Creole mother is so attached, dies in the fire; and between the fire and the death, her mother breaks down and ultimately goes mad.

Among the significant objects that embody Antoinette's West Indian childhood is 'the picture of the Miller's Daughter'. Those who know Third World society will understand or remember such bits of Europe, on calendars, notebooks, picture books; they seem to lack any organic connection, but symbolise a dominating foreign presence which is so much part of the landscape of one's life that their incongruity is after a while hardly noticed. Yet, this foreign presence is always shaping standards to which those living 'on the periphery', away from where things 'really happen', must aspire.

All that is familiar entirely destroyed; all the beauty which hid the brutality burnt away. One last hope appears: her Black friend, the daughter of her mother's servant:

> Then, not so far off, I saw Tia and her mother and I ran to her, for she was all that was left of my life as it had been. We had eaten the same food, slept side by side, bathed in the same river. As I ran, I thought, I will live with Tia and I will be like her. Not to leave Coulibri. Not to go. Not. When I was close I saw the jagged stone in her hand but I did not see her throw

> it. I did not feel it either, only something wet,
> running down my face. I looked at her and I saw her
> face crumple up as she began to cry. We stared at
> each other, blood on my face, tears on hers. It was
> as if I saw myself. Like in a looking-glass. [p.45]

Divided from Tia, she is divided from herself. At this
moment of powerlessness, she sees reflected in Tia both
sides of her dilemma, clearly and simultaneously: in Tia's
tear-stained face and in the stone she has thrown; in Tia's
attachment to her and rejection of her; all this has been
revealed by the act of burning down the Great House.

Here I believe is the source of the peculiar vulnerability
of Jean Rhys's heroines in previous novels. The woman,
the foreigner, the alien, always the same person, is
taken by European readers to be European, prefiguring
later novels and plays of the isolated and rootless by
Existentialists.

But Jean Rhys's heroine is not European. She is West
Indian. And though she is white, she is less the descendant
of Hester, her English stepmother, than of Francine, her
West Indian mammy. Tia is her sister under the skin. And
divided from Tia by the history of slavery and the racial
chasm, this woman begins life divided from herself. In
the novels she wanders through Europe, first as a young,
then as an older, and finally as an ageing woman, but
never able to mobilise herself to fight back. It is because
she is divided at the root of her being that she lacks the
strength, the sustenance, the positive confirmation of her
right to survive, to be autonomous, to flourish. As a
woman she is particularly under attack; as a woman she
has no wife or girlfriend to mitigate her loss and to
confirm her life right.

Her dilemma as a woman is one with her dilemma as a
white West Indian. The separation of race and sex as
political categories has limited use when they are aspects
of one personality, in fiction and in life. These two

aspects of herself shed light on each other and empha-
sise the grossly uneven balance of power the heroine is
always up against.

The Jean Rhys heroines, isolated and alienated, are even
now taken to be European by some; by others, their
feminism is kept at a safe distance from their preoccupations with race. But they are not European; and their
concentration on the female dilemma and on female
vulnerability with men and in society generally is inseparable from the West Indian preoccupations about race of
their creator.

Jean Rhys is a West Indian woman writer, in perception,
in preoccupation and in prose. ('Not to leave Coulibri. Not
to go. Not.') While these two strands were divided in
earlier work, in *Wide Sargasso Sea* Ms. Rhys is able to
put them together for the first time. They strengthen
and reinforce each other. Neither is a metaphor or symbol
for the other; both demand joint resolution.

Antoinette is raised in convents and learns to live with
her tragedy. She grows into a beautiful woman and
inherits a fortune from her English stepfather when he
dies. Rochester, the second son of an English Great House,
has no money of his own; he therefore must find money to
marry where he can. His father sends him to the West
Indies to find a Creole heiress, as was not uncommon in
the nineteenth century, and he finds Antoinette.

He does not love Antoinette Bertha Cosway. He has
married for money, not love. But unlike the *woman* who
marries for money, the money he marries becomes his.
Once he has it, he sets out to destroy his wife.

He resents her local associations, her only independent
source of power. He feels hostility from this strange
tropical place of which his wife is a part. It is still shaped
by wild tropical beauty; still aware of more than the
rational, still in contact with creative impulses not mediated by money. And so is she. These embarrass him, make
him the stranger, and challenge him as a man and

as a European. Ms. Rhys has him speak for himself:

> . . . everything around me was hostile . . . The trees
> were threatening and the shadows of the trees moving
> slowly over the floor menaced me. That green
> menace. I had felt it ever since I saw this place. There
> was nothing I knew, nothing to comfort me. [p.149]

He feels these people have some secret he cannot know,
and that his wife shares it with the servants; she is like
them, part of them, not his.

> . . . the feeling of something unknown and hostile
> was very strong. 'I feel very much a stranger here,' I
> said. 'I feel that this place is my enemy and on your
> side.' [p.129]

The Sargasso Sea has sharpened but not invented the
division between them. Men are often threatened by the
independent power base of the women they marry.
Rochester defends himself by evoking the social power he
has as a man and as a European to vent his hostility on
Antoinette. He renames her. He refuses to call her
Antoinette and instead calls her Bertha. Here is the
European identifying the Third World woman; here is the
man defining his wife. He succeeds in his campaign of
attack; she is entirely defeated and he calls her defeat
madness. The effort exhausts him, and only then does he
tell us how he defines sanity:

> All the mad conflicting emotions had gone and left
> me wearied and empty. Sane. [p.172]

Earlier he has described his childhood:

> How old was I when I learned to hide what I felt? A
> very small boy. Six, five, even earlier. It was
> necessary, I was told, and that view I have always
> accepted. [p.103]

It is this acceptance of repression, this 'sanity', that has defeated Antoinette. He takes her to England where he is entirely in charge, thanks to her money, and then he locks her away; she is driven to madness by that.

Antoinette is locked in the attic for some years, with a guard, Grace Poole, from whose policing she is always trying to escape. We are back in the pages of the Gothic novel, but we come to it having traversed the globe: from England to the West Indies and back again. This time the imprisonment is not a device to evoke terror, since it is not more terrible than all that went before. Rather, it symbolises the actual power balance in an old and ongoing conflict of interests between the sexes and between the Third World and the metropolis.

Over the years, Antoinette has a recurring dream which is never complete. The first time she has it she is still in the West Indies, and on each of the other two occasions, more of the story is revealed. She is always trying to find out what she is supposed to do, and she is always going somewhere with a stranger. The first time:

Someone who hated me was with me . . . [p.26]

The second time, she is —

. . . following the man who is with me . . . I follow him, sick with fear but I make no effort to save myself . . . [p.59]

She sees a flight of steps, the top of which is her destination. She has the dream again after years of being locked in the Great House:

That was the third time I had my dream, and it ended. I know now that the flight of steps leads to this room where I lie watching the woman asleep with her head on her arms. [p.187]

Sometimes when Grace Poole falls asleep or drinks herself to sleep while on duty (because it's a lonely job ensuring other people's loneliness), Antoinette, this insane

Mrs. Rochester, escapes.

> In my dream I waited till she began to snore, then I
> got up, took the keys and let myself out with a candle
> in my hand. It was easier this time than ever before
> and I walked as though I were flying.
>
> All the people who had been staying in the house
> had gone, for the bedroom doors were shut, but it
> seemed to me that someone was following me,
> someone was chasing me, laughing. Sometimes I
> looked to the right or to the left but I never looked
> behind me for I did not want to see that ghost of a
> woman whom they say haunts this place. [p.187]

The 'ghost' is herself; she has heard them talk about her
without knowing it was she they were talking about. But
it is also the person she has been — a ghost — being
discussed by the person she is becoming. She is no longer
the passive victim. She acts. She is not 'sane' like
Rochester; she does not accept repression. She fights
against it. The protagonist has exorcised the ghost of the
victim. Finally. But she has not left the past behind;
instead she will remember what this victim found out in
her captivity:

> At last I was in the hall where a lamp was burning. I
> remember that when I came. A lamp and the dark
> staircase and the veil over my face. They think I
> don't remember but I do. [pp. 187-8]

Even those whose history has never been chronicled have
a long memory.

> There was a door to the right. I opened it and went
> in. It was a large room with a red carpet and red
> curtains. Everything else was white. I sat down on a
> couch to look at it and it seemed sad and cold and
> empty to me, like a church without an altar. I wished
> to see it clearly so I lit all the candles, and there were

> many. I lit them carefully from the one I was
> carrying but I couldn't reach up to the chandelier.
> Then I looked round for the altar for with so many
> candles and so much red, the room reminded me of a
> church. Then I heard a clock ticking and it was made
> of gold. Gold is the idol they worship. [p.188]

She is beginning to understand now what motivates the
strange people whose voices have come from the other
side of the attic door over the years, and who have
imprisoned her. They are motivated by money. Jane
Austen knew that.

Antoinette feels miserable in the room and is afraid of
being discovered. (All of this, you remember, is her dream.)
But she is not discovered, and she sinks back on to a couch.
Then in her mind's eye she is transported back home:

> Suddenly I was in Aunt Cora's room. I saw the
> sunlight coming through the window, the tree outside
> and the shadows of the leaves on the floor, but I saw
> the wax candles too and I hated them. [p.188]

It is tragic for her to have this manufactured substitute for
the natural sunlight from which she has been taken. She
hates England, she hates the metropolitan world, she hates
the cold and the damp, she hates the household in which
she has been imprisoned, and she hates the personification
of all this, her husband Rochester. All of her anger now is
focussed on the artificial light of the candles.

> So I knocked them all down. [p.188]

Now that is not only, You must take my word, or, You
must accept my feelings. This is a woman saying, This is
how I feel and this is what I'm going to do about it. This
is 150 years after Elizabeth Bennet. If the candles bother
me, I'll knock them down.

> I laughed when I saw the lovely colour spreading so
> fast, but I did not stay to watch it. I went into the

hall again with the tall candle in my hand. It was then that I saw her — the ghost. The woman with streaming hair. She was surrounded by a gilt frame but I knew her. I dropped the candle I was carrying and it caught the end of a table-cloth and I saw flames shoot up. As I ran or perhaps floated or flew I called help me Christophine help me and looking behind me I saw that I had been helped.

[pp. 188-9]

Christophine was her Black mammy in the West Indies, who tried to help her but whose mystic powers were not enough to save Antoinette from Rochester because she was too white. It is to Christophine that she has always gone for help. She receives her help again, and goes on:

There were more candles on a table and I took one of them and ran up the first flight of stairs and the second. On the second floor I threw away the candle. But I did not stay to watch. I ran up the last flight of stairs and along the passage. I passed the room where they brought me yesterday or the day before yesterday, I don't remember. Perhaps it was quite long ago for I seemed to know the house quite well. [p. 189]

We have known the Great House for a long time, those of us in England, those of us in the United States, those of us in the West Indies.

I knew how to get away from the heat and the shouting, for there was shouting now. [p.189]

Now, we remember the scene when her own Coulibri was burnt down. Then she had said:

. . . they roared as we came out, then there was another roar behind us. [p.41]

This time she hears the shouting, not in terror, but in tranquillity, the first she has known.

> When I was out on the battlements it was cool and
> I could hardly hear them. I sat there quietly. I don't
> know how long I sat. Then I turned round and saw
> the sky. It was red and all my life was in it. [p.189]

She has been burning this house down and by that act her
whole life is coming to her, coming together, finally. Not
only that room, but everything that she has lived through,
as a woman, as a white West Indian, as an immigrant
to Britain. Now she begins to face her past, the past of the
descendant of the slave owner, the daughter of one Great
House and the wife of another.

> I saw the grandfather clock and Aunt Cora's patch-
> work, all colours, I saw the orchids and the stepha-
> notis and the jasmine and the tree of life in flames.
> [p.189]

The West Indies is fire itself in these images — confirming and
encouraging her in what she is doing in this England place.

> I saw the chandelier and the red carpet downstairs
> and the bamboos and the tree ferns, the gold ferns
> and the silver, and the soft green velvet of the moss
> on the garden wall. I saw my doll's house and the
> books and the picture of the Miller's Daughter. I
> heard the parrot call as he did when he saw a
> stranger, *Qui est là? Qui est là?* [in her native tongue,
> Creole — derived from the French] and the man
> who hated me [Rochester] was calling too, Bertha!
> Bertha! [p.189]

To the last he would identify her, but she has already
moved beyond his reach. Only his voice is left as a presence.
She is now *identifying herself.* From being the object of
Rochester's power, Antoinette is transforming herself into
the subject, by grasping the power to determine her own
actions and her own fate.

> The wind caught my hair and it streamed out like

wings. It might bear me up, I thought, if I jumped
to those hard stones. But when I looked over the
edge I saw the pool at Coulibri. Tia was there.
[pp. 189-90]

She is still dreaming, and in her dream she is home again,
on the plantation that had burnt down around her, not
the one she is burning down around herself. And Tia is
there, the Black child who was her friend, and from whom
she was divided; Tia, who rejected her to go for her own
power, is home with her.

She beckoned to me and when I hesitated, she
laughed. I heard her say, You frightened? And I
heard the man's voice, Bertha! Bertha! [p. 190]

Here are her two choices. On the one hand Rochester, who
has driven her sanity from her, dragged her from her home
and imprisoned her in a shrine to gold; Rochester is calling
Bertha back to his control. And on the other hand Tia,
the Black girl, her people, her childhood friend who
embodies her personal history and her social history as a
West Indian; Tia beckons and invites Antoinette to join her
and be free of this man.

All this I saw and heard in a fraction of a second.
[The truth is often hidden for centuries and then
bursts upon us in an intense moment.] And the sky
so red. Someone screamed and I thought, *Why did I
scream?* I called 'Tia!' and jumped and woke. [p. 190]

She wakes now that she has decided between them.[28]

* * *

Now something happened between Jean Rhys's writing of
novels in the twenties and thirties and her writing of this
novel in the fifties (it was first published in 1966). What
happened was, first, a massive movement for Third World

independence and, secondly, a massive West Indian immigration into Britain. Her people had come — the Tias and the Francines and the Christophines — and they were stronger than they had been when she left them in the West Indies in the early part of this century. She would have heard English racism against them — she was rediscovered by Francis Wyndham in 1958, the year of the Nottingham and Notting Hill riots against Black people; and she would have felt that she herself was under attack. But she would not have felt alone. This was a new source of power finally to confront all the misery and isolation and loneliness that she had worked to record and articulate in her earlier novels. She had been an outcast as a woman, she had been an outcast as a West Indian, she had been an outcast as a white West Indian. She ended her novels in defeat because she herself was born in defeat. Now another power enters her writing arm. As a result, her heroine is no longer the passive victim that history has tried to make her. Antoinette is now able to move against the arrogant, racist and brutal metropolis and against the arrogant, racist and brutal man who personifies it — Mr. Rochester. Many years before, she had said, 'I will live with Tia and I will be like her.' But first she had to let Tia know the terms on which she planned for them to be together. All she had offered Tia before was the domination of her white skin. But as Antoinette burns down the Great House which imprisons her — as Tia had burnt down the Great House which was the centre of her exploitation — Tia welcomes her home.

The Great House. Sir Thomas Bertram's Great House which ruled his plantations in Antigua. All the forces he repressed finally come together in their effort to ford the wide Sargasso Sea — his wife and his slaves — and they burn him down.

Antoinette wakes from the dream.

Grace Poole was sitting at the table but she had

heard the scream too, for she said, 'What was that?'
She got up, came over and looked at me. I lay still,
breathing evenly with my eyes shut. [Like every
prisoner she is lying to her jailer.] 'I must have been
dreaming,' she said. Then she went back, not to the
table but to her bed. I waited a long time after I heard
her snore, then I got up, took the keys and unlocked
the door. I was outside holding my candle. Now at
last I know why I was brought here and what I have
to do. [p.190]

'Now at last I know why I was brought here and what I
have to do.' The dreams were premonitions. Her voyage
to Europe was her destiny. Rochester was the obstacle
to Tia, who was the goal.

We now approach a more realistic ending to Jane
Austen's novels. Jean Rhys has said her heroine, a West
Indian, a white woman, was 'brought here' to burn
Rochester's England down. And when she does, there is
another West Indian, a Black woman, waiting for her
because that's what she wants to do too. The reason that
Ms. Austen's novels could only end by skipping away from
the problems they posed was that each heroine was isolated
in her room at the top. Jean Rhys's heroine works out her
conflicts with Rochester always in the consciousness of
where she has come from, always drawing on the power,
at least in imagination and dream, of Christophine and Tia.
In the end, that is why she can convincingly win against
him.

As literature comes from life, so literature must return
to it. I end with a passage not from a novel, but by a
woman, a Black woman. Her name is Margaret Prescod.
She was born in Barbados. Her ancestors could have been
on one of Sir Thomas Bertram's plantations. She now lives
in the United States. I quote from the final paragraphs of
her fine book on women's experience of emigration and
immigration.[29]

This is the last round in destroying this mammy image, this mammy role, this mammy work. Often we're told that we have an option, that if you don't want to be a mammy, you can be a 'lady'. But we've already learnt something from the white women who are now saying plenty about this 'lady' business. [And have been saying so since Jane Austen put her pen to paper.] Not only that, but we've never forgotten what we knew about the ladies when we were cleaning their houses or in slavery. They were coming to *us* for advice about how to deal with *their* situation. And we saw how they were freaking out and quite often we had to hold them together. We learned a lot about what this dependency on the men did to them. So we don't want that stuff either.

So we're rejecting the mammy image and rejecting the lady image, and the ladies and the mammies are coming together.

Here is the true ending of Jane Austen's novels. But of course this is not fiction. The last fictional word is still to come. It is the whole story of the Great House from the point of view of Tia, and Black women have begun to write it.

Notes

1. (page 11) '. . . the real basis of professionalism is the capacity both to exclude others from having access to specialised knowledge, scientific or unscientific, *and* to "specialise" common knowledge — to convince others that they can't possess that knowledge and must be dependent on the professional. A member of a profession can charge more for his skills because he is organised to prevent competition.' From 'The Home in the Hospital' by the Power of Women Collective, in *All Work and No Pay* edited by Wendy Edmond and Suzie Fleming, Falling Wall Press, 1975, p.69.

This view now pops up more often and in unexpected places: 'The assumption is that we professionals know best and should take charge. There is precious little justification for this belief, and indeed the weight of the evidence is rather to the contrary. The professional classes seem intent on annexing ever larger areas of life and making them their private preserve. This seems to me of questionable value to society, and simply betrays the patronising authoritarianism behind the liberal's facade of concern.' From a letter to the *Guardian*, 10 August, 1983, by Dr. Rob

Poole, London SW4.

Both of the above refer to the medical profession, whose professional habits are increasingly being exposed as a danger to life and limb. But the critique has general application, which does not preclude either doctors or literary critics from being selfless and dedicated to their skills or from making remarkable and important contributions to our lives and our pursuit of happiness. (Sometimes these are *despite* their professions.)

2. (page 12) '. . . as soon as the distribution of labour comes into being, each man has a particular, exclusive sphere of activity, which is forced upon him and from which he cannot escape. He is a hunter, a fisherman, a shepherd, or a critical critic, and must remain so if he does not want to lose his means of livelihood . . .' From *German Ideology* by Karl Marx and Frederick Engels, Moscow, 1968, p.45. They propose a society where it is possible 'to do one thing today and another tomorrow, to hunt in the morning, fish in the afternoon, rear cattle in the evening, criticise after dinner, just as I have a mind, without ever becoming hunter, fisherman, shepherd or critic.'

3. (page 14) The phrase is from D.W. Harding's very fine essay in *Scrutiny* (Vol. VIII, No. 4, March 1940), 'Regulated Hatred: An Aspect of the Work of Jane Austen'.

Later in this book I use Mr. Harding's discovery that Jane Austen hid devastating comments amidst her less disturbing prose. I found this discovery invaluable. It was also in 1940 a major breakthrough against the traditional reduction of Jane Austen to a cleverly critical supporter of the aristocracy. David Cecil's *Portrait of Jane Austen* (Constable, 1978), with his reduction of Ms. Austen to Gentle Jane, is more typical of Lord David than of the majority of her readers. He has his own reasons for ignoring her savagery against the ruling class in the nineteenth century.

I now wonder about the degree of self-censorship by
the reader then, when a minority of the population was in
cities, unlike now. The technique of slipping in such
savage comments certainly allowed the reader to choose
to ignore such a critique of her world. But to be living
among 'a neighbourhood of voluntary spies', Mr. Harding's
famous example of a hidden Austen bomb (from *Northanger Abbey*), is very much taken for granted in a small
community, which allows itself to think and even to
verbalise some very harsh and caustic judgements about
neighbours. In my experience, the nineteenth century
English countryside that Ms. Austen describes resembles
any small non-industrial community, especially one not
dominated by radio and/or television (as in parts of the
Third World). While many aspects of life may be mystified by the superstitions in such a rural community, there
are some aspects of everyday life which are refreshingly
obvious and some facts of life that are taken for granted
and spoken about more freely than in a city. (The
question, by the way, which might today come to
the city reader's − or any reader's − mind is: on behalf of which bureaucracy are these neighbours spying
voluntarily?)

4. (page 15) See note 3 above.

5. (page 16) *Jane Austen's Letters*, collected and edited
by R.W. Chapman, Oxford University Press, second edition,
London, 1979, p. 401.

6. (page 19) It was no less a person than Count Leo
Tolstoy who expressed this reactionary view most brazenly.
He quotes what he considers 'a remarkably wise and profound thought' from one M. Ata that '. . . the trouble [with
women trying to prove they can do what men do] is that
men cannot do anything even approximately approaching

what women can accomplish.' He then comments:

> Yes, that is certainly so, and it is true not only of the
> bearing, nursing, and early education of children, but
> men cannot do what is loftiest, best, and brings man
> nearest to God — the work of loving, of complete
> devotion to the beloved, which has been so well and
> naturally done, and is done and will be done, by good
> women.

(From an Afterword to Chekhov's story, 'Darling', in *What Is Art? and Essays on Art*, Oxford University Press, London, 1930.)

There are at least two lessons to be learnt here, neither of which the Count intended. The first is to be suspicious of *any* praise of *any* 'special' or 'natural' or 'instinctive' qualities women supposedly have. Such praise is almost always an excuse for condemning us to the work men don't want to do, and withholding from us what we demand which men don't want to give up.

The second lesson is about art. While Count Tolstoy the man may have had these reactionary views, in *Anna Karenina*, the creation of Leo Tolstoy the writer, Anna's devotion to 'the work of loving' leads her to be far from a 'good' woman — to be a rebel who refuses to love her husband. Further, Tolstoy's point in *The Death of Ivan Illyich* is precisely that it is men's refusal to do 'the work of loving' which can ruin their lives and even their deaths. An artist's views on subjects other than her/his art can be as absurd or reactionary as anybody else's. When s/he creates however, it is as though s/he switches into another gear in the brain: another process takes over which is dependent on perception rather than precept.

This fact has been noted before. Unfortunately, the artist's gifts are sometimes used to excuse the artist's prejudices; or at least to excuse others from the responsibility of calling the artist on these prejudices as one would call 'ordinary' people. None of us can afford to allow such racism as for example Count Tolstoy's against women.

7. (page 22) *A Room of One's Own*, Granada, London, 1977. She states her case:

> Intellectual freedom depends upon material things. Poetry depends upon intellectual freedom. And women have always been poor, not for two hundred years merely, but from the beginning of time. Women have had less intellectual freedom than the sons of Athenian slaves. Women, then, have not had a dog's chance of writing poetry. That is why I have laid so much stress on money and a room of one's own. [p. 103]

8. (page 23) This is a method that some of us in the women's movement share with many artists and particularly those who aim to sell their art to a popular audience. F. Scott Fitzgerald spells it out in his unfinished *The Last Tycoon* (Grey Walls Press, London, 1949). Stahr, the last of the great movie moguls, is told in casual conversation with a stranger fishing on the beach that 'I never let my children go' to the movies. After the conversation, the man 'went off over the beach toward the road, unaware that he had rocked an industry.' (p. 111)

Days later, Stahr realises that he is on the verge of a creative breakthrough about what movies and what kind of movies to make:

> . . . he listened inside himself as if something by an unknown composer, powerful and strange and strong, was about to be played for the first time. The theme would be stated presently, but because the composer was always new, he would not recognize it as the theme right away. It would come in some such guise as the auto horns from the technicolour boulevards below, or be barely audible [as] a tattoo on the muffled drum of the moon. He strained to hear it, knowing only that music was beginning, new music

that he liked and did not understand. It was hard to react to what one could [not] entirely compass — this was new and confusing, nothing one could shut off in the middle and supply the rest from an old score.

Also, and persistently, and bound up with the other, there was the negro on the sand. He was waiting at home for Stahr, with his pails of silver fish, and he would be waiting at the studio in the morning. He had said that he did not allow his children to listen to Stahr's story. He was prejudiced and wrong, and he must be shown somehow, some way. A picture, many pictures, a decade of pictures, must be made to show him he was wrong. Since he had spoken, Stahr had thrown four pictures out of his plans — one that was going into production this week. They were borderline pictures in point of interest, but at least he submitted the borderline pictures to the negro and found them trash. And he put back on his list a difficult picture that he had tossed to the wolves, to Brady and Marcus and the rest, to get his way on something else. He rescued it for the negro man. [p.114]

The artist or the organiser does not allow her audience to determine what she feels. But she does open herself entirely to the audience telling her how much — or how little — they know about their own feelings; how much of their own feelings they can face and articulate themselves. This focuses her creative energy on finding the method and shaping the form of conveying what she has to say, which in turn clarifies and refines her own feelings, her own content. Such a dialogue with the audience is one of the most creative aspects of movement politics.

It is worth noting here that while Virginia Woolf was preoccupied with women and money in her non-fiction (see especially *Three Guineas*), it was Scott Fitzgerald who tackled the effects of money as a major fictional theme, and who did it brilliantly in *The Great Gatsby* and *Tender is the Night*. In each, the characters divide between those who use money to use people and those who are forced by lack of it to be used. Of the latter, one man dies and the other goes mad. Scott Fitzgerald is no feminist – in both books 'the rich' are women – but he has plenty of value to say. Ms. Austen and Fitzgerald show that spelling out the power of money is not itself corruption; rather, this is the best guarantee of working out how to build defences against those who use it against you.

9. (page 23) In *The World As We See It* (CCIC [Arts Section] 1977), to celebrate International Women's Decade, Gertrude Elias wrote in her short piece, 'Art and Money':

> . . . A recent study of artists' incomes revealed that artists engaged in the visual arts range on the bottom of the social scale. The income of 'successful' artists was put at no more than £2,000 a year.
>
> The precariousness of the profession can be assessed when one considers that such outstanding a painter as L.S. Lowry thought it too risky to rely on an income from his pictures, and kept his job as a rent collector until his age of retirement at sixty-five.

Probably a job not even then open to women. Ms. Elias's visual work is as clear and blunt as these comments.

10. (page 23) 'A Critical Theory of Jane Austen's Writings' by Q.D. Leavis: *Scrutiny*, Vol. X, No.1, June 1941; II. '"Lady Susan" into "Mansfield Park"', Vol. X, No.2, Oct. 1941; II. '"Lady Susan" into "Mansfield Park" (ii)', Vol. X, No.3, Jan. 1942; III. 'The Letters', Vol. XIII, No.2, Spring 1944.

Ms. Leavis's account is in my view more inside the way Jane Austen worked, and the way she viewed her work, than anyone except Virginia Woolf, in a sense Ms. Austen's heir (Ms. Woolf was, like her, profoundly concerned about women and money – see notes 7 and 8 above and 19 below). Ms. Leavis's combination of scrupulous scholarship and housewifely common sense opens the way for her deductions and perceptions to fuse into a brilliant whole. She allows the artist some ordinary humanity, which contributes greatly to genuine respect for Jane Austen while avoiding the adulation that makes her inaccessible and sets her up to have her intentions mystified.

11. (page 24) I'm told that Ms. Leavis would advise her students to 'read whenever you can, in every spare moment' – or words to that effect. That was the only way to do the work of criticism. She was most likely describing the way to survive that she had worked out for herself. In this respect Jane Austen was lucky: much of *her* research took place in drawing-rooms, watching and listening, and then comparing notes with her room-mate, sister Cassandra.

12. (page 26) What 'changing ourselves' actually means is another subject. For example, hundreds of women's groups (c-r groups among them) sprang up almost overnight then, calling themselves 'Women's Liberation'. This stirred all kinds of opposition, support, questions, debates, new situations and new relationships – it began to change the world. The power of being effective in this way helped women immeasurably in their individual efforts to change, and helped those changes to 'take': women could more easily sustain the changes they were making in themselves because by organising they were changing the balance of power in the society – they were changing everyone. It was much more than talk that made the c-r group effective.

How much we can change ourselves when the basic situation for women does not substantially alter is a more difficult question, which was a subject of Ms. Austen's novels. For example, she hoped that women could marry for love but she knew and spelled out that none of us can live on love. Was it weakness or shrewd practicality when Charlotte Lucas, Elizabeth Bennet's clever friend, agrees to marry Mr. Collins? After all, Charlotte will never have her own home except through marriage to him. Ms. Austen never tells us definitely what she thinks. All she says is that Elizabeth was confused at first, but later understood it better.

The women's movement has had a hard time with this question too, often unable to distinguish between what are personal weaknesses in other (often less privileged) women, and the range of tactics — however compromised they appear — which women use to survive. All too often feminists miss the distinction between when women are weak and when they are in a weak social position.

13. (page 28) This is one of the points made by Suzie Fleming in her Introduction to the forthcoming republication of Eleanor Rathbone's *The Disinherited Family* (Falling Wall Press, Bristol, 1984). Ms. Nightingale was a great protagonist of financial independence for women.

14. (page 28) It was not only nunneries that provided an alternative to marriage. In Belgium there is the beguinage, a cluster of small houses round a cathedral for the daughters of the wealthy, who thus lived in the shadow but not the clutches of the Church. The beguinage dates from about the sixteenth century, and would have provided a respectable 'refuge for lesbian and other rebellious women to live apart from and independent of the family, and in a community of women. In a Protestant country such as England, the Church was less of a sexual choice, though Karen Armstrong, in *Through the Narrow Gate* (Pan Books, London, 1982), makes clear it was one for her.

15. (page 35) *The Complete Poems of Emily Dickinson*, edited by Thomas H. Johnson, Faber & Faber, London, 1970, p.94. My thanks to my dear old friend Filomena D'addario for introducing me to the wonders of Ms. Dickinson.

16. (page 38) Quoted in *Beyond a Boundary* by C.L.R. James, Hutchinson, London, 1963, p. 161.

17. (page 41) Frances Anne Kemble's *Journal of a Residence on a Georgian Plantation in 1838-1839* (edited by John A. Scott, Knopf, New York, 1961) is a contribution to an informed judgement about these women: the work they did and the bold fight at least some of them made on behalf of slaves. Fanny Kemble fought on behalf of women in particular.

Ms. Kemble was English and an established actress, so she was able to divorce her slaveholding husband, and return to England and the stage. This no doubt accounted for some, but by no means all, of her boldness.

18. (page 50) Mr. Rochester, in explaining to Jane Eyre why he married Bertha Antoinette (which Ms. Rhys has transformed into Antoinette Bertha, putting her Creole name first — see Part II), says to her: 'Her family wished to secure me because I was of a good race . . .' (*Jane Eyre* by Charlotte Brontë, Penguin, London, 1966, p.332). If there is any doubt about whether this is also *his* view of race, a few pages later, speaking of his life since his wife's madness, he spells it out: 'Hiring a mistress is the next worse thing to buying a slave: both are often by nature, and always by position, inferior . . .' Charlotte Brontë does not disapprove; she has Jane say: 'I felt the truth of these words. . .' (p.339)

19. (page 51) Patricia Beer in *Reader, I Married Him* (Macmillan, London, 1974) says: 'Significantly, the only

person who utters anything like feminist sentiments is
Mrs. Elton, the half-educated vulgarian in *Emma*!' (p.45)
Mrs. Elton's lack is not of education but of sensibility,
loyalty, generosity — every one of what are considered
classic human virtues. Such a mean personality cannot be
the source of feminist sentiments in an Austen novel; and
if Ms. Beer had looked more closely, she would have seen
that the words bely the sentiment; that is precisely the
author's intention. To Ms. Beer, it seems, even Emma's
unsentimental analysis of the pecuniary motives for
marriage is not feminist enough.

It becomes even clearer that Ms. Beer's view of what
constitute 'feminist sentiments' is distorting her judgement
of Jane Austen's work when she says of Anne Elliot's
dismissal of male writers in *Persuasion* (quoted above) that
Ms. Austen does not attach to her words 'any kind of
resentment and rebellion.' (p.45) In 1817 (even in 1917),
stating this was rebellious enough. And in any case, Anne
is resentful, even if her quiet way of expressing it
doesn't measure up to Ms. Beer's standards. On the
contrary, I believe that feminism necessarily involves every
woman's right to express herself in her own style, and
that while resentment is a spur to feminist struggle, it is not
its aim.

The problem is that Ms. Beer's assumptions are hostile
to Ms. Austen's, and not because Ms. Austen is not a
feminist. Ms. Beer again: whereas the Austen heroines 'for
the most part live unthinkingly on the labour of others',
'paid employment' in Charlotte Bronte's work brings her
heroines 'face to face with the Woman Question'. (p.86)
Presumably the 'Woman Question' is not to be found with
the woman at home, only in 'paid employment'.

Jane Austen's heroines are certainly from the upper
classes and do not clean their own or other people's
homes. But they do work. Being a lady is work. Being a
wife and daughter is work. Being hostess, companion,
emotional supporter, mother, in the home and under the

domination of tyrants, is work. (Virginia Woolf, whose *To the Lighthouse* describes some of that work in detail, thought women married to the upper class should be given a wage for doing it, which would give them the financial independence to refuse to do it and to refuse war – see her *Three Guineas*.) As long as some feminists see only women in paid employment as protagonists, or at least as more than parasites, the housework that poor women do and the housework of the dependent wives and daughters of wealthy men will both remain visible. (Fortunately such a view is already on the way out in other spheres of the movement.)

Patricia Stubbs (*Women and Fiction: Feminism and the Novel 1880-1920*, Methuen, London, 1979) has a similar socialist realist aesthetic. Her ideal seems to be H.G. Wells, whose utopian novels Virginia Woolf attacked. Ms. Woolf was as suspicious of Mr. Wells's reforming fiction as I am of Mrs. Elton's reforming rhetoric. His books, she said, 'leave one with so strange a feeling of incompleteness and dissatisfaction. In order to complete them it seems necessary to do something – to join a society, or, more desperately, to write a cheque . . .' ('Mr. Bennett and Mrs. Brown', quoted in *Women and Fiction*, p.180). That is how one expects to react to a political tract: guilt is not the aim of creative fiction.

For Ms. Stubbs, however, Ms. Woolf should have followed Mr. Wells's prescription of what the novel was to accomplish. But her 'frigidity [sic sic sic] may have something to do with' her not having made any 'coherent attempt to create new models, new images of women.' (p.231) This is exactly the criticism I have heard feminists level at Ms. Austen. Ms. Austen's and Ms. Woolf's (and every great novelist's and indeed artist's) work exposes the reality hidden in the old despised or at least neglected and underestimated 'models', and demonstrates all the new and subversive potential that is repressed there. It never aims to be a sociological or political exercise in setting examples of approved 'role models'.

20. (page 53) George Lamming, *Natives of My Person*, Longman, London, 1972. In *Of Age and Innocence,* a Black man explains to a white woman the personal experience that turns him into a nationalist leader. On the other hand, the white woman has discovered she has lesbian feelings. Mr. Lamming's analogy between how it feels to be Black and how it feels to be lesbian; and his phrase, 'in spite of', to express how it feels for others to make allowances for your 'inferiority', are unequalled, and, sadly, neglected in the women's movement.

21. (page 54) Mozart's piano concertos often have deeply tragic slow movements, but only two, K466 and K491, have last movements which attempt an emotional resolution of what the first two movements have posited.

22. (page 55) I appreciated the value of stepping outside of the ordinary routines when I participated with the English Collective of Prostitutes and other women's organisations in the Occupation of the Church of the Holy Cross, London (17-29 November, 1982). We slept on the floor of an unheated church which had no cooking facilities. This is how I wrote about it:

> Our lives had literally stopped for 12 days: the milkman had not been paid, the post not collected and the money not earned. We were physically exhausted and we craved a bath and a bed. Yet we were loathe to re-enter the flat atmosphere of daily life. We dreaded slipping away from the authentic and collective life inside the church, back into the harness and blinders of daily routines.

(To be published in the anthology, *Feminist Action,* edited by Joy Holland, Battle Axe Books, London, 1984.)

23. (page 57) Ford Madox Ford in 'Preface to a Selection of Stories' from *The Left Bank* (Jonathan Cape, 1972),

reprinted in *Tigers Are Better-Looking*, Penguin Books, London, 1972, p.138. Here is the rest of the sentence:

> . . . she has let her pen loose on the Left Banks of the Old World − on its gaols, its studios, its salons, its cafes, its criminals, its midinettes − with a bias of admiration for its midinettes and of sympathy for its lawbreakers.

24. (page 61) Introduction to *Wide Sargasso Sea*, p.11.

25. (page 61) Ibid.

It is worth recording how Jean Rhys felt about her rediscovery. When in 1966 she got the W.H. Smith Award for *Wide Sargasso Sea*, she commented, 'It has come too late'. If she had been recognised earlier, she might have made another life for herself. The reason she was not rediscovered earlier, or even was lost in the first place, has to do with the nature of the English literary Establishment. The great (like Jane Austen) are approved for the wrong reasons or (like Jean Rhys) approved too late and for the wrong reasons.

For example, A. Alvarez in the *Observer* (20 May, 1979), said Ms. Rhys is 'one of the finest British writers of this century'; and in reviewing *Wide Sargasso Sea* originally in the *New York Times Book Review* (quoted in the *New York Times*, 17 May, 1979, by Herbert Mitgang), he said that she was 'quite simply, the best living English novelist . . .'

Ms. Rhys was a West Indian. That is what she is fighting to establish in *Wide Sargasso Sea*. To deny her that is to call her Bertha when her name is Antoinette (see below).

Mr. Alvarez then went on to say that 'although her range is narrow, there is no one else writing who combines such emotional penetration and formal artistry or approaches her unemphatic, unblinking truthfulness.' My case is made: women are always said to provide a narrow range; as I wrote in another context, men's 'wider' range is 'never wide enough to include us'. Ms. Rhys's attempt to penetrate the most crucial divisions of our time, those of sex, race and class, is entirely overlooked. It is enough to break a writer's heart and to inspire a movement among the readers.

26 (page 61)   See the passage quoted in note 18.

27 (page 62)   *The Pleasures of Exile*, Michael Joseph, London (1960).

28 (page 72)   Edward Kamau Brathwaite, the very distinguished poet from the West Indies, has commented on this crucial passage in *Contradictory Omens* (Savacou Working Paper Reprint 1, Mona, Jamaica, 1982, p.36):

> The 'jump' here is a jump to death; so that Antoinette wakes to death, not to life; for life would have meant dreaming in the reality of madness in a cold castle in England. But death was also her allegiance to the carefully detailed exotic fantasy of the West Indies. In fact, neither world is 'real'. They exist inside the head. Tia was not and never could have been her friend. No matter what Jean Rhys might have made Antoinette think, Tia was historically separated from her by this kind of paralogue . . . [and he quotes a passage which makes abundantly clear the racism of the white West Indian].

Wally Look Lai of Trinidad in 'The Road to Thornfield Hall' (*New Beacon Reviews*, Collection One, edited by John La Rose, London, 1968) responded differently:

> . . . Antoinette's act of burning Thornfield Hall down, and her leap from the battlements, far from being acts of self-destruction, were attempts to do the very opposite: to save herself from an existence which had become a form of death, and to restore to her life the

> only possibility which she had come finally to see as
> capable of leading to fulfilment . . . Antoinette's leap
> was her first attempt to take command of, and
> redirect, the forces which had hitherto dictated the
> direction of her life . . .

I quote so extensively because the question is vital: can
Black and white women join together, or is the Sargasso
Sea which divides us so wide and so deep that Ms. Rhys's
fictional representation of the joining must remain only
fiction?

If cultural differences are what divide us, then women
would never be with men, so different are the 'personal and
group attitudes, behaviour and perception' (p.48) of the
sexes — women's culture from men's. This is why
Antoinette had to get away from Rochester. (For another
definition of culture, its relation to the divisions among us,
and how to approach destroying these divisions, see my
Sex, Race and Class, Falling Wall Press, 1975.)

I don't believe that 'Tia was not and never could have
been [Antoinette's] friend.' The hatred which is produced
by the divisions of sex, race, class, age, nation, etc., has
never been able to stamp out communication, even love,
between us, and never will. What is decisive is that Jean
Rhys *did not have Tia jump to Antoinette, but Antoinette
to Tia*. As women have waited for men, so Black women
have waited for white women — and for everyone.

George Lamming concludes *Natives of My Person* (see
note 20 above) with the wives who are waiting for their
men (whom they do not know are dead) discussing why
they wait. One woman explains: 'We are a future they must
learn.' Women do wait for men to learn — but we do not
passively wait; we act against them and speed up the
education process! I do not believe that any of us waits for
those who have oppressed us, quietly hoping for them to
change. We act and force them to change.

Tia's people, Black people, burnt Antoinette's Great

House to the ground. That was the beginning of the education. I believe that is 'real'. Rochester's cruelty is also 'real'.
Antoinette acts and burns down Rochester's mansion. That
is why Tia, who has always been waiting, finally welcomes
Antoinette; for Antoinette has met her conditions: her first
leap is to burn down Thornfield Hall. Jumping to Tia is the
logical second leap.

Mr. Look Lai implies that in the context of what was
possible for Antoinette, jumping to her death was a
victory. I agree.

Again I refer to George Lamming's work, this time to
Of Age and Innocence, where the West Indian myth of the
Tribe Boys, and their massive jump into the sea when they
could not defeat the slavemasters any other way, is
recorded as the triumph it was. Suicide, in literature and
life, can also be an act of defiance.

Wide Sargasso Sea is a novel, a creation, a fiction. Its
relevance to life is demonstrated by the heat generated in
this debate about 'jumping to Tia'. In the final analysis,
whatever Jean Rhys meant or did not mean, whatever
Antoinette or Tia did or did not do, we cannot allow, on
pain of mass destruction, that the Sargasso or any other sea
should keep us apart. Jean Rhys's vision must be of the
future reality.

29. (page 74) *Black Women: Bringing It All Back Home* by
Margaret Prescod-Roberts (now Prescod) and Norma Steele,
Falling Wall Press, 1980. With the kind permission of
Margaret Prescod, I edited her last paragraphs to suit my
purpose.

A Last Note

In the course of writing this book, I appreciated Jean Rhys
in a new way. *Wide Sargasso Sea* has 190 pages of words,
and each one was weighed and considered in relation to
every other in a way that I have never seen except in a

poem. It *is* a poem, and, to paraphrase its author, all her life was in it.

How much this is literally true can be seen from her unfinished autobiography, *Smile Please* (1979). From the portrait of her mother and their antagonistic relationship, to her descriptions of Black people, and her own feelings of being an outcast among white and Black, even to the vegetation, the parrot, the patchwork quilt — the West Indian terrain of *Wide Sargasso Sea* is shown to be drawn from her own life there. I believe this is because Ms. Rhys, from childhood in the West Indies and adulthood in Europe, had many scores to settle and her creation of Antoinette was for the purpose of settling them. She wanted to burn down all that Rochester symbolised on her own behalf as a West Indian woman, and she wanted us to know.

In the original Charlotte Brontë story of Jane Eyre, the heroine's name was Mason. Ms. Rhys gives Antoinette another name so that both her mother and father are Creole and the European Mason is the stepfather. The name she gives her is Cosway — or causeway, the bridge between the Third World and Europe, between one race and another, a causeway from defeat to victory. I believe it is a triumph for us as women, for all of us as citizens of the world.

Publisher's Note: Following her speech at the Cheltenham Literary Festival, Selma James was invited to speak on 'The Ladies and the Mammies' in Chicago in March 1980. The talk was videotaped and edited. It is suitable for use in schools, colleges, conferences, etc.

The videotape can be shown in two parts with an interval: *Part I — Jane Austen* (about 30 mins.), *Part II — Jean Rhys* (about 15 mins.).

This is a Woman unLimited Production, available on VHS ¾" cassettes and Betamax ½" cassettes (black and white) from:

    UK   Housewives in Dialogue, King's Cross Women's Centre,
             71 Tonbridge Street, London WC1 (tel: 01-837-759)

    US   Boston Wages for Housework Committee, Box 94,
             Brighton, MA 02135

Appendix:
A Definition of Mammy

Mammy is a mythologised Black woman, a glorification of an actual historical figure from the time of slavery in the United States. She is portrayed as a large woman with a round face and a scarf tied around her head — like Aunt Jemima on a box of pancake mix, someone whom a white child was able to turn to for everything. No matter what the pains of existence, she was the woman who always had a sweet for him if he wanted something sweet. If he fell down and hurt his knee or had a squabble with his mother, this Mammy was somebody he could run to, someone constantly picking up the pieces, and even after he grew up, she was always there for him to confide in: the person who had really raised him when his white mother had not.

The Mammy image suggests that in the midst of the mess of the white family, the plantation master's family, there was a Black woman who was a pillar of stability, who kept everything together, who was always good-tempered, who had the solution to every problem, a person who couldn't possibly have existed. But the glorification of Mammy was rooted in the reality that as a slave, Mammy

had to work hard and well and with the utmost for-
bearance — her alternative was the lash. So Mammy did
protect; she did mediate; she did take care.

The Mammy, as distinct from the Black concubine, the
nubile slave girl, the 'Negress', was de-sexualised —
according to the myth, her fulfilment in life came from
serving the white family.

The Mammy image helps project white women onto a
pedestal, as the feminine ideal Black women could never
reach. It also implies that the white woman was too fragile
to raise her own children. If we were doing all the nasty
work of taking care of children and cleaning the house,
then what did white women do? They could fix themselves
up; they weren't ruining their hands with manual labour.
They weren't going barefoot. The Mammy image makes
the white woman look very insubstantial, languishing on
balconies sipping mint juleps. But most white women were
never in that position. Even the ones who were sipping the
mint juleps — what was going on behind that? The collabo-
ration that must at least sometimes have gone on between
white women and Black women is hidden by the Mammy
image (and by the image of the Southern lady).

But at the same time Mammy was a slave, so there must
have been another side. Her hostility and revenge might
not have been directed at the white child but were perhaps
directed through the child at the master and the mistress.

Part of the disappointment and bitterness associated
with Mammy is that the reward for the work she had put
in didn't ever come. She continued as a slave, and when she
got too old to serve the white family, she was put out.
Frederick Douglass talks about his grandmother who was a
Mammy. Once she got too old to work, the master just put
her out in a house where she was isolated and was not
being taken care of. She didn't have enough food, she
didn't have anybody to work for her, she was alone. He
used to run away to be with his grandmother, to have that
time with her. After having put in all that work, she didn't

get anything.

Mammy was also the pain of the attention that a mother was compelled to give to somebody else's child — and what was denied her own child at the same time. She was taking care of a white child, and yes, she did build up a relationship with that child and she did love that child and she was involved in the growth of that child. But at the same time her own child would not be allowed to learn how to read whereas she saw this child reading; her own child didn't have enough to eat, whereas the white child had plenty to eat.

On the other hand, a lot of Mammies used the power they had from taking care of white children to get all kinds of advantages for their own children. Their children could play with white children and learn how to speak English in a certain way, how to read and write. The Mammy was in a position to manipulate the power balance on the plantation in favour of Black people, partly by persuading white people by example — more likely shaming them into admitting — that Black people were human. Mammy was the living contradiction to all the racist stereotypes and myths against Black people, that we were sub-human, that we were stupid, that we were savages. All the lies of slavery were contradicted by the fact that Mammy, a Black woman, was entrusted with raising the child of the plantation master.

W.B.B.

Excerpt from Sharpening the Mother Tongue: The New Women's Dictionary *edited by Ruth Todasco, to be published in 1984 by Falling Wall Press.*